DICTIONARY OF
ETHICAL AND LEGAL
TERMS AND ISSUES

THE ESSENTIAL

GUIDE FOR

MENTAL HEALTH

PROFESSIONALS

LEN SPERRY

Routledge
Taylor & Francis Group
New York   London

Routledge is an imprint of the
Taylor & Francis Group, an informa business

Routledge
Taylor & Francis Group
270 Madison Avenue
New York, NY 10016

Routledge
Taylor & Francis Group
2 Park Square
Milton Park, Abingdon
Oxon OX14 4RN

© 2007 by Taylor & Francis Group, LLC
Routledge is an imprint of Taylor & Francis Group, an Informa business

Printed in the United States of America on acid-free paper
10 9 8 7 6 5 4 3 2 1

International Standard Book Number-10: 0-415-95322-7 (Softcover) 0-415-95321-9 (Hardcover)
International Standard Book Number-13: 978-0-415-95322-1 (Softcover) 978-0-415-95321-4 (Hardcover)

Library of Congress Cataloging-in-Publication Data

Sperry, Len.
    Dictionary of ethical and legal terms and issues : the essential guide for mental health professionals / Len Sperry.
        p. ; cm.
    Includes bibliographical references and index.
        ISBN 0-415-95321-9 (hb : alk. paper) -- ISBN 0-415-95322-7 (pb : alk. paper)
        1. Psychiatric ethics. 2. Forensic psychiatry. 3. Psychiatric ethics--Dictionaries. 4.
Forensic psychiatry--Dictionaries.   I. Title.
        [DNLM: 1. Psychiatry--ethics. 2. Psychiatry--legislation & jurisprudence. 3.
Ethics, Professional. 4. Terminology.   WM 21 S751d 2007]

    RC455.2.E8S655 2007
    174.2--dc22   2006014597

Visit the Taylor & Francis Web site at
http://www.taylorandfrancis.com

and the Routledge Web site at
http://www.routledgementalhealth.com

CONTENTS

ACKNOWLEDGMENTS

The decision to plan, write, review, revise, and publish a professional book is a long and complex process involving multitudes of individuals besides the stated author. I've been extraordinarily blessed to have teamed up with the visionary publishing director at Routledge, George Zimmar, Ph.D., who immediately grasped the potential value of the concept of this book and worked with me to fashion and refine it into its present form. Thanks, George.

Over the past few years I've had the opportunity to share ideas about ethical and legal practice with several colleagues and I would like to recognize them: Michael Gottlieb, Ph.D., Dennis Engels, Ph.D., Mike Robinson, Ph.D., James R. Bitter, Ed.D., Maureen Duffy, Ph.D., Carl Chan, M.D., Joe Layde, M.D., J.D., Michael Frain, Ph.D., Larry Kontosh, Ph.D., Alex O. Miranda, Ph.D., Paul R. Peluso, Ph.D., Bill Nicoll, Ph.D, Greg Brigman, Ph.D., and Linda Webb, Ph.D. Furthermore, a number of highly regarded ethics and legal scholars have taken the time to review the manuscript and I extend a heartfelt gratitude to them. They include Laura Roberts, M.D., Thomas Plante, Ph.D., and Ronald Bullis, Ph.D., J.D.

I am most grateful for the collaboration and contribution of Colette Corcoran, J.D., a licensed mental health counselor who is completing her Ph.D. at Florida Atlantic University. Ms. Corcoran's expertise in the practice of family law and mental health is evident in her major contribution to Part III of this book. My appreciation is likewise extended to Katherine Hendricks, a research assistant at the university, who helped in the preparation of parts of an early draft. Finally, I'd like to acknowledge the wonderfully talented editorial and production team at Routledge—Fred Coppersmith, Dana Bliss, Michael Washburn, and Takisha Jackson—who ensured that the final version was professional in every respect.

INTRODUCTION

The professional practice of counseling and mental health has become overly complex and litigious. Public outcry over recent corporate and government scandals has led to a proliferation of litigation and has fueled calls for increased ethics training and accountability for management professionals. Not surprisingly, scrutiny of ethical practice has extended beyond business and government to all professional sectors, including the mental health profession. Recently, the mental health professions have pledged to increase the ethical sensitivity and competence of their members in response to increasing litigation aimed at mental health providers. These professional organizations also have recently updated and expanded their codes of professional practice to reflect the demand for greater accountability. Accordingly, all counseling and mental health students—as well as practitioners who are already certified or licensed—are required to have formal ethics training (a graduate course or a continuing education seminar) and demonstrate some level of ethical sensitivity and competency. Although there are currently several professional ethics textbooks, there are few, if any, supporting resources to assist students and practitioners in mastering basic terminology and accessing important legal opinions regarding legal and ethical dilemmas in everyday practice.

Other than the rare professional ethics text that has a glossary of terms, students and mental health professionals are essentially left to their own devices when they need to find the meaning of an ethical or legal term. They may frantically flip through a textbook hoping to find a definition and often are frustrated to find that although terms are described and illustrated over a few paragraphs, seldom are the terms authoritatively defined in a phrase or sentence. Or, hoping to find a concise analysis of ethical or legal issues or an explanation of a legal statute or case law, they search through a general law resource guide or text only to find that general law dictionaries and general legal reference texts do not summarize key legal cases relevant to their professional needs. Again, they feel frustrated by the lack of relevant resources.

What is needed is a fingertip resource guide that includes the key terms, a concise guide to the key ethical and legal issues and considerations, codes and statutes, and the key legal opinions (case law) and key legislation and regulations relevant to everyday mental health practice in the United States. The *Dictionary of Ethical and Legal Terms and Issues: The Essential Guide for Mental Health Professionals* meets that need.

The book is divided into three parts. Part I includes all the ethical and legal terms necessary for engaging in everyday practice. Parts II and III provide the reader with a concise description and guidelines for the most common ethical and legal issues and considerations.

Because the language of ethics and law tends to be rather technical, Parts II and III have been made as user-friendly as possible. Accordingly, key terms relevant to each ethical or legal issue are provided in the discussion of each ethical and legal topic. In addition, implications and applications of each topic are described and practical guidelines for dealing with each issue or consideration are provided.

These two parts are designed so that the reader can turn to a particular topic and get a full description, including definitions of key terms involving the topic, in one place. Thus, instead of having to go from Part II or Part III to search through Part I for the definitions of one or more of related terms, these terms are all included for each of the specific ethical or legal issues discussed in Parts II and III. For example, if the reader were to consult the issue of the Boundaries, Boundary Crossings, and Violations in Part II, he or she would find a section of related key terms useful in understanding this issue. These terms include boundary, categorical boundaries view, dimensional boundaries view, boundary crossing, boundary violation, conflict of interest, and dual or multiple relationships, which form the basis of the discussion of the complex issue of boundaries in professional mental health practice. This special feature was included to spare the busy student and practitioner time and hassle. Finally, an appendix provides a brief summary of relevant court rulings and legislative enactments regarding a wide range of ethical and legal matters impacting the professional practice of counselors and other mental health professionals.

This book will be of interest to students in graduate programs in counseling, psychology, marriage and family therapy, psychiatry, nursing, and social work, as well as to students in undergraduate programs in human services who need a ready reference for myriad ethical and legal terms and issues that they are expected to know in both coursework and practicum and internship training. It also will be of value as a ready reference source to mental health practitioners.

A word on terminology: Instead of referring to mental health professionals and others with titles such as counselor, therapist, psychotherapist, psychiatrist, clinician, or school counselor, the generic term "practitioner" is used to refer to all such professionals providing mental health and other counseling services.

Part I

Dictionary of Ethical and Legal Terms

abandonment
A practitioner's unilateral discontinuation of needed services to a client without reasonable notice. Also refers to discontinuation without provision for or referral to adequate treatment.

abuse (adult)
Nonaccidental infliction of physical, sexual, social, or emotional harm or of economic exploitation of an adult. Some jurisdictions require mandatory reporting of such actions for older adults, that is, those over the age of 65.

abuse (child)
Nonaccidental infliction of physical harm to a child, continual psychological damage, or denial of emotional needs (neglect). Cf. *adverse childhood experiences.*

abuse allegation
A charge of abuse of an individual of a legally protected class, for example, child, disabled, or elderly.

academic accountability
The obligation to demonstrate academic, career, and/or personal/social outcomes resulting from student participation in school counseling programs.

accommodation
Cf. *reasonable accommodation.*

accreditation
The process whereby a professional educational program voluntarily undergoes review by a recognized accrediting body and is found to meet its standards for quality.

accrediting bodies
Organizations that review and certify that professional educational programs meet specific academic and/or practice standards. APA, CACREP, and ACSW accredit academic mental health and related programs.

actionable
Giving rise to a "cause of action." Something or a situation for which a suit may be filed.

ADA
Cf. *Americans with Disabilities Act.*

administrative agency
A government body charged with administrating or implementing specific groups of legislation.

administrative law
Regulations and procedures that govern the operation of administrative agencies.

administrative safeguards
Safeguards required by HIPAA that limit access to protected health information to those authorized and to prevent those who are unauthorized, whether workforce members or others, from obtaining access to electronic protected health information. For example, an employer might allow only practitioners rather than all employees to have access to the computer files that contain diagnostic information or progress notes.

admissibility
Refers to whether a court is bound to receive or permit introduction of a particular piece of evidence, in accord with the requirements of the law of evidence.

4

adoption
The process in which ties to biological parents are legally voided or canceled and new legal ties to adopting parents are created.

advance directives
Written instructions, often called a living will, expressing individuals' health-related wishes in the event they become incapacitated and are unable to make such decisions for themselves. It may include a durable power of attorney, which gives someone else the right to make such decisions. For example, an individual may wish to refuse being fed through a tube or may wish not to be resuscitated once dead. Also referred to as advance care directives.

adverse childhood experiences (ACE)
A term that encompasses abuse, neglect, exposure to family violence, and other forms of childhood adversity.

adversarial system
A system of law in the United States wherein the truth is believed to be best revealed through a contest in court between opposite sides of a dispute.

advocacy
The active espousing or pleading in favor of a legal position. The professional duty a lawyer has in the representation of a client. In legal proceedings, mental health expert witnesses should present their opinions objectively rather than plead the cause of a client. This differs from the duty of advocacy expected of a treating practitioner who pleads the interests of his or her patient/client.

affidavit
A voluntary statement of facts or a voluntary declaration in writing that an individual affirms or swears to be true before an official authorized to administer an oath.

affirmative defenses
Defenses recognized by the law, which, when introduced by defendants in a trial, will reduce or eliminate responsibility for acts.

agency liability
The legal theory holding that all individuals in an "agent" relationship can be held vicariously liable for each other's official acts.

agent
An individual who represents or acts on behalf of another or an organization with a mutual agreement to do so.

alienation of affections
A civil wrong or tort that arises from the willful and malicious interference with a marriage relationship by a third party. This claim can be raised when a practitioner doing couples therapy is accused of interfering with a patient's marriage.

alimony
Payments, temporary or permanent, that a court may order one spouse to make to another.

allegations
Unproven claims that a person has violated a law or is liable for wrongfully harming another individual personally or financially. Charges in a criminal indictment and the accusations in a civil complaint are referred to as allegations.

alternative counseling
Approach to counseling that involves interventions and models of treatment that are outside the usual and conventional purview of professional counseling practice.

alternative medicine
The utilization of medical or healing methods and interventions that are outside the usual and customary pattern of medical practice in place of conventional or mainstream medical interventions. Differs from complementary medicine.

American Mental Health Counselors Association (AMHCA)
The primary professional body overseeing the practice of professional mental health counseling.

American School Counselor Association (ASCA)
A professional organization whose membership consists of certified/ licensed in school counseling and others with unique qualifications and skills to address the academic, personal/social, and career development needs of students.

Americans with Disabilities Act (ADA)
Federal legislation enacted in 1990 that bars employers from discriminating against disabled persons in hiring, promotion, or other provisions of employment, especially in the provision of reasonable accommodation in response to their disability.

amicus curiae
Literally, a "friend of the court." One who has an indirect interest in a case and offers or is requested to provide information to the court in order to clarify particular matters before the court. A position paper filed in court by that individual or organization is referred to as an amicus curiae brief.

amnesia
A medical or psychological condition that results in the inability to recall all the relevant aspects of an event that one can reasonably be expected to recall.

analytical ethics
Branch of general or philosophical ethics that studies the nature of morality itself. Sometimes referred to as "meta-ethics."

annulment
A legal or religious decree that a marriage never existed. A court hearing to determine whether an annulment should be granted is called an annulment proceeding.

applied ethics
The division of ethics that focuses on cases or situations and uses them to understand or develop standards, rules, and theories. Applied ethics is subdivided into professional ethics, clinical ethics, organizational ethics, environmental ethics, and social and political ethics.

Aquinas, Thomas
Medieval philosopher (1225–1274) whose major treatise, *Summa Theologica,* was a systematic synthesis of Christian theology based on his extension of the work of Aristotle. His ethical system is teleological, meaning that an individual always acts with a specific end (telos) in view, and that the telos is always good and that the highest good is God. Thus, for Aquinas, God stands at the heart of ethics.

arbitrating
A process wherein a negotiator or negotiators seek the judgment of individuals in resolving a dispute.

arbitration
An alternative dispute resolution process occurring outside a courtroom. Decisions made by arbitrators may or may not be binding on participants; however, decisions made in "binding arbitrations" are binding on participants.

Aristotle
Greek philosopher (384–323 B.C.) who developed the first systematic treatise on ethics, called *Nicomachean Ethics.* Contended that ethics begins with the search for the highest human good, which is happiness, that is, eudaemonia, the result of a life of virtuous activity lived in accord with reason. Proposed the "golden mean" standard wherein excellence consisted in moderation in all matters and that virtue lies between deficit and excess. Cf. *eudaemonism.*

arraign
To accuse someone of a wrong by a process of law. It is the first step in the criminal accusation process, at which the defendant is formally charged, informed of his/her rights, offered an opportunity to plead, and provided with counsel if he or she can afford none.

aspirational ethics
Ethical values and principles that greatly exceed minimal, prescribed ethical values and principles, which are referred to as mandatory ethics.

aspirational professional standards
Standards of professional practice that exceed the minimum standards mandated by a code of professional ethics. Standards that are deemed compatible and consistent with achieving positive and healthy outcomes for clients, practitioners, and the mental health professions as a whole.

assault
An intentional act or threat designed to make another fearful and reasonably apprehensive of harmful or offensive contact.

assent
The process of consulting with and informing a client regarding his or her preferences about actions to be taken by the practitioner. This process

fulfills the practitioner's ethical obligations to the client with regard to informed consent.

assessment
The process that involves the collection and evaluation of information to address a client's counseling or rehabilitation concern or problem. Usually, clients are assessed against a normative standard, or a set of criteria, for the purpose of achieving a diagnosis, planning treatment, or implementing interventions.

assignment
The process of transferring rights, responsibilities, or property from one party to another. The assignee is the one to whom those privileges are given or assigned, whereas the assignor is the one who does the assigning.

assisted suicide
The voluntary provision of assistance in the suicide of an individual (normally with a terminal illness) who chooses to end his/her life.

assumption of risk
An act in which an injured (possibly injured) party knows he/she might be injured but voluntarily puts himself/herself at risk anyway.

attachment theory
A psychological theory that posits that parent-child attachment is influenced by innate variables and that many responses of infants, such as crying and clinging behavior, are innate instead of learned. This theory has been influential in court decisions that grant physical child custody more to mothers than to fathers.

autonomy
The ethical value and principle of taking responsibility for one's own behavior and self-direction; freedom to choose without interfering with others' freedom. In a counseling context, it refers to the right of clients to determine their own thoughts, actions, and futures, and to regulate their own behavior.

balancing
The weighing of opposing principles for the purpose of making the best judgment.

bartering
Practice of acceptance of goods, services, or other nonmonetary remuneration from clients in return for clinical or counseling services.

battered child syndrome
Psychological and/or behavioral conditions resulting from systematic abuse and/or neglect of a child. Evidence of an abnormal pattern of emotional, physical, and behavioral reactions or adaptations shown by a child, which is attributable to the abuse experienced.

battered person syndrome
Psychological and/or behavioral conditions resulting from systematic abuse and/or neglect of an adult. An abnormal pattern of emotional and behavioral reactions or adaptations is shown by the person, which is attributable to the abuse experienced.

battered wife syndrome
Psychological and/or behavioral conditions resulting from systematic spousal abuse. An abnormal pattern of emotional and behavioral reactions or adaptations is shown, which is attributable to spousal abuse. Also referred to as battered woman's syndrome.

battery
Intentional harmful or offensive touching of one individual by another without the consent of the individual being touched. It need not result in physical injury, and may exist even if only an extension of the individual is touched. Practitioners should note that in the absence of informed consent, treatment could be considered battery.

beneficence
The ethical value and principle that guides actions consistent with contributing to the well-being of others. This value implies doing good to others.

benevolence
The ethical value of being altruistic and caring, sharing, helping, and acting generously toward others.

best interest of the child
A legal test that seeks to achieve the best interests of a child involved in a judicial or administrative hearing. It is applied in custody, adoption, termination of parental rights, and child support matters.

beyond a reasonable doubt
The highest standard of proof required to convict an individual of a crime. It represents probability in the range of 95% to 98% that the crime was committed by that individual and that is used only in criminal cases. It compares with "clear and convincing evidence" with a probability of 70%-plus that is used in both criminal and civil cases, as well as "by a fair preponderance of the evidence" with a probability of at least 50% that is used exclusively in civil cases.

billing
The practice by which the practitioner informs the client and third party payor, if applicable, on an ongoing basis of the amount that is owed for services rendered and by whom.

biomedical ethics
Applied ethics that focuses on aspects of the biological sciences, medicine, and health care. A way of understanding the complexity of biomedical research as applied to medicine and health care in terms of religious or moral values.

borrowed servant rule
Situation in which there is both a general employer (called the master employer) and another employer (called a special employer) and in which only one is deemed the employer for purposes of liability. For example, in the context of a university training program wherein a supervisee is under the supervision of both a university supervisor and a supervisor at an off-site agency, the university supervisor could be considered the master employer and the agency supervisor could be considered the special employer. This creates the possibility for the general or the special employer to escape liability. In evaluating whether the general or special employer should be liable, the court will look to which party had the ability to control the supervisee at the time of the act.

boundary
The frame and limits surrounding a therapeutic relationship that defines a set of roles and rules for relating for both client and practitioner. Because of a power differential between client and practitioner, and because clients are in a vulnerable position, adequate boundaries serve to protect the client's welfare. The concept of boundary is central to understanding conflicts of interest and involves two polar positions: the categorical boundaries view and the dimensional boundaries view, wherein boundary crossings and boundary violations are a major point of contention.

boundary crossings
A benign and typically beneficial departure from traditional expectations about the settings and constraint of clinical practice. They involve any deviation of clinical behavior from the standards of practice associated with traditional or conservative treatment approaches that emphasize emotional distance or reducing clinical risk and liability. Accompanying a phobic client in riding up and down in a small elevator during exposure therapy or greeting a South American client with an embrace—a culturally sensitive practice—are examples. Such crossings are commonly accepted in many humanistic, behavioral, and systemic forms of psychotherapy. There is evidence that boundary crossings may promote both the therapeutic alliance and positive client outcomes.

boundary violations
Exploitive or harmful practices in psychotherapy that occur when practitioners cross standards of professional behavior for their own sexual, emotional, or financial gain. Examples include becoming sexually

involved with a client, entering into a business partnership with a client, or confiding personal information to a client to satisfy the practitioner's own emotional needs.

breach of contract
Failure to provide contracted or agreed-on services.

breach of duty
The failure by a professional to perform a legal duty imposed by professional ethics, statute, or case law. One of the grounds for filing a malpractice lawsuit.

brief
A written summary prepared by one side in a lawsuit to explain its case to a judge.

burden of proof
Requirement that facts or evidence must demonstrate that the matter being considered actually occurred and that the facts asserted are in accordance with rules of evidence. In a criminal trial, the burden "beyond a reasonable doubt" (extremely sure, generally 95–98%); in most civil trials, a mere "preponderance of the evidence" (just over 50%); and, in some civil settings, such as child custody and most civil commitments, "clear and convincing evidence" (over 70%) is used.

burnout
An emotional state experienced by some practitioners; characterized by an emotional exhaustion in which the professional no longer has any positive feelings, sympathy, or respect for clients.

business ethics
Application of ethical categories and principles to the unique circumstances and responsibilities of business and management.

capacity
The ability to make a rational decision or give informed consent.

capital offense
A criminal offense that is punishable by death in some jurisdictions.

captain of the ship doctrine
The doctrine that holds a physician responsible for the negligent acts of other professionals because he/she had the right and duty to control and oversee the overall care provided to the patient.

care ethics
The ethical theory that is rooted in persons and relationships, wherein ethical decisions are made by focusing on relationships rather than on actions, duties, or consequences. An act is considered morally good and right if it expresses care or is done to maintain a caring relationship.

case citation
A means of accessing a court's opinion in a particular case. Such a citation identifies the parties involved in the case, the source or text in which the case is found, the court writing the opinion, and the year in which the case was decided.

case consultation
A process of conferring with a knowledgeable, competent professional to obtain a second opinion or advice on an issue or issue concerning a particular case. Also referred to as expert consultation.

case law
Law derived by a judge based on previous cases or precedents. A primary source of legal authority that parallels statutory law.

case management
A process in mental health care that primarily focuses on maintenance of the positive results of care. The use of therapeutic techniques, consultation, follow-up, testing, and professional collaborations to avoid a client's decompensation or deterioration.

case manager
An individual who focuses on interviewing, planning rehabilitation, medical, or educational programs; coordinating services; interacting with significant others; placing clients in facilities, organizations, or jobs; following and monitoring a client's progress; and solving problems.

categorical boundaries
The view that boundaries are part of human interaction with the purpose of delineating role functions and of facilitating the therapeutic process. In this view, boundaries in professional relationships are considered immutable, not open to debate, and should not be crossed for any reason. Furthermore, such boundary crossings are viewed as a slippery slope, which eventually results in serious boundary violations.

categorical imperative
Refers to the supreme or most basic principle in duty ethics or deontological ethics. Immanuel Kant posited that right actions flow out of right principles and right principles should govern all situations. He articulated this imperative in various ways, one of them being: "Act in such a way that you always treat humans not merely as means to an end but also as an end."

casuistry
Ethical approach to analyzing moral and legal that argues from the abstract to the particular and applies abstract or universal ethical principles to specific, unique cases. In this approach, ethical reasoning about a problematic case starts by focusing on a paradigm case, that is, a consensus case wherein circumstances are clear and there is little or

no ambiguity about its rightness or wrongness. Ethical decisions are then made by exploring similarities and differences of the problematic case to the paradigmatic one. Although there are several paradigm cases in bioethics, currently there are very few involving counseling and psychotherapy, thus limiting the application of this approach to mental health practice.

certification
A voluntary means of identifying oneself as a trained and qualified specialist in counseling, clinical psychology, or other professions. Certification usually requires meeting national standards of expertise beyond those required for state licensure. Counselors who meet the standards of the National Board for Certified Counselors (NBCC) are awarded the designation National Certified Counselor (NCC), whereas clinical psychologists who meet the standards of the American Board of Professional Psychology are awarded a diploma in clinical psychology (ABPP-CL) and can represent themselves as "board certified."

character
That which gives orientation, purpose, and shape to one's life. In classical ethics, it is the cluster of virtues that makes an individual what he/she is. In contemporary ethics, it includes the capacity for reason and choice, which endows individuals with moral and social responsibility for their actions.

child abuse
Harmful conduct with a minor, including sexual, physical, or emotional abuse, and/or severe neglect of a child's basic needs for food, clothing, shelter, and medical treatment. It is a crime and mental health professionals must report—known as mandatory reporting—it in accordance to their state law. Cf. *adverse childhood experiences.*

child custody
Cf. *custody.*

child protective service
An administrative agency charged with implementing child protection laws of a state.

child sexual abuse accommodation syndrome
A clinical syndrome wherein an abused child denies that the abuse occurred. Also called child abuse accommodation syndrome.

child support
Payments made by one parent to the other parent for the maintenance of the child or children of those parents.

child witness
A minor testifying in the legal proceeding.

circumstantial evidence
Evidence that can indirectly prove a main fact in question. Because it is inferential, such evidence is open to doubt.

civil action
A noncriminal action presented in a court for the purpose of gaining or recovering civil rights or compensation for an individual.

civil court
A court that hears civil lawsuits. These include domestic, landlord-tenant, personal injury, business disputes, and real estate cases.

civil law
The body of law that describes the private rights and responsibilities of individuals to one another. It involves actions filed by one individual against another such as divorce actions or workers' compensation claims.

civil rights law
Specific groups of laws that give or affirm specific civil rights for all or for specific groups of citizens. For example, wrongful commitment of an individual to an inpatient psychiatric unit would be in violation of that individual's civil and constitutional rights.

class action
Legal action brought by one or more individuals on behalf of themselves and others who are impacted by the same illegal act.

clear and convincing evidence
The second level of proof utilized in both civil and criminal cases. It is the standard often used in hearings concerning involuntary confinement of the mentally impaired.

client assistance program
A publicly funded program that advocates for the consumer in situations in which there is a discrepancy between the needs and wants of the consumer and the services of the state vocational rehabilitation program.

clinical ethics
The branch of applied ethics that focuses on all aspects of ethics involving health care delivery, research, and policy.

clinical privileges
Permission granted by an institution, such as a hospital or clinic, to a qualified professional to perform professional duties. Usually requires the screening of qualifications, diploma, licensure, and past professional record.

clinical supervision
The evaluative and directive oversight provided by a more senior mental health professional to a more junior one, which extends over time. Its purpose is to improve the junior's professional functioning, to monitor the quality of services provided to clients, and to serve as a gatekeeping function for the profession.

code
A systematic and specialized compilation of laws or statutes, usually having an index to facilitate locating pertinent provisions.

collaborative decision making
Decisions are made in a cooperative manner by practitioners and their client and client's family and/or social network. Such decisions are typically about the nature of treatment, options to treatment, treatment effectiveness, and termination of treatment.

common good
Normative standard for evaluating the justice inherent within social, legal, and political actions within a community. Based on the idea that to the extent an act benefits the entire community it is fair and just. It is always in tension with the rights of individuals.

common law
A system of law wherein legal principles are derived from case law or usage and custom as expressed by the courts rather than from statutes. A body of legal principles that have evolved and continue to expand from court decisions.

common law marriage
A type of marriage relationship based on living together and acting as if married in the eyes of the community. Many jurisdictions do not permit or sanction such marriages.

community
Group of individuals who share one or more normative designations that are geographical, political, ethnic, spiritual, or moral. It has a unique culture and set of values that inform its ethical attitudes and actions.

community property
Property acquired during a marriage that is viewed as belonging to both spouses. Usually, this property is divided evenly in a divorce. Also called marital property.

community values
Refers to the ideals, beliefs, norms, and ethos in a given community.

compensatory damages
Damages awarded to reimburse the injured party for the actual loss incurred. Cf. *punitive damages.*

competence (client)
The capacity of clients to make decisions about their own well-being; a necessary condition for informed consent.

competence (practitioner)
The capacity of practitioners to provide a minimum quality of service within their scope of practice. For legal purposes, competence is evaluated by what other reasonably prudent practitioners in the same community would do under the same circumstance.

competency to stand trial
The ability of an individual to understand and rationally participate in a court proceeding.

complaint
A formal pleading made in behalf of the complainant to a court demanding relief and informing the defendant of the grounds of the suit.

complaint (ethical)
A formal grievance by an individual, called a complainant, that expresses dissatisfaction with a practitioner's action, and appeals to the professional organization that one or more of its ethical standards have been violated.

complementary and alternative counseling
Approach to counseling that involves alternative counseling interventions that are utilized alongside or in conjunction with usual and traditional counseling interventions. Designated as CAC.

complementary and alternative medicine
A recent term that blurs the distinction between alternative medicine and complementary medicine. It often is designated as CAM.

complementary medicine
The utilization of alternative medical or healing methods alongside or in conjunction with conventional medical interventions.

compliance
Following professional treatment directives.

comprehension
Having sufficient information and the capacity to understand it. Understanding the risks and benefits of services under consideration is a prerequisite for a client giving fully informed consent.

compulsory treatment
Counseling or therapy that is initiated or demanded by a third party, usually as a form of rehabilitation or for the ongoing assessment of a client.

confession
An admission of guilt.

confidential communication
A disclosure by a person to another, which is intended to remain secret. It may be legally defined and protected. It usually applies to communications between clients and professionals.

confidential information
Information received from a client or research participant by a mental health professional acting in a professional role.

confidentiality
The obligation of practitioners to respect the privacy of clients by not revealing to others the information communicated to them by the client during counseling sessions unless released by the client to do so. In couples and family therapy, it is granted primarily to the couple or whole family rather than to the individual, unless otherwise stated.

conflict of interest
Conflict between loyalties or duties to a client possibly resulting from multiple roles with a single client. Arises when a practitioner has competing interests that interfere with faithfully exercising his/her professional judgment and skill in working with clients. Also can arise where the supervisor has competing interests that may interfere with the supervisor's duty to faithfully exercise his/her professional judgment in working with the supervisee.

conformity
The following of rules and observation of societal regulations.

consequential ethics
The ethical theory that aims at realizing the best possible consequences. An act is considered good and right only if it tends to produce more good consequences normatively weighted than bad consequences for everyone involved.

conservator
An individual appointed by a court as the legal representative of a mentally ill or incompetent person. A conservator has the power to protect and control the property of an incompetent person and the power to restrict the movements and actions of that individual who becomes the ward of the conservator.

conservatorship
The legal entity arranged and administered by a conservator to protect and restrict an incompetent person.

consultant
An individual providing consultation. The consultant's professional relationship is with the consultee—usually a practitioner or administrator who contracts for the consultant's services—rather than with the patient; thus, a practitioner-patient relationship does not form.

consultation
A formal arrangement wherein a practitioner obtains a second opinion, advice, or supervision on an issue or issues of concern from a knowledgeable, competent colleague.

consultation confidentiality
A professional understanding, contract, or agreement with the client that extends practitioner-client confidentiality to the consultant.

consumer
A term used in place of client or patient by some mental health professionals, particularly rehabilitation personnel, in order to show the choice that the person with a disability has in the process.

contempt of court
A violation of a court order that is punishable by fines and/or jail. A contempt citation is a legal notice that an individual has violated the orders of a court and that penalties will be applied.

contingency fee
A fee for services that depends on the outcome of a case. Such a fee is usually considered unethical for forensic expert witnesses and consultants.

contract
A legal agreement that can be written, oral, or implicit in the parties' behavior. Failure to honor the agreement is a breach of contract and can be grounds for a lawsuit.

contract law
The body of law governing contracts.

contributory negligence
Negligence by the injured individual, which when combined with the negligence of the professional results in the proximate cause of the injury. A more contemporary legal doctrine is contributory fault that permits the apportionment of damage based on the percentage of the fault of both parties.

copayment
Amount required by some insurers to be paid by the client to the practitioner in addition to that which is by the third-party payor or insurance company.

corporal punishment
An act of physical force upon a child or student for the purpose of punishing the child or student.

Council for Accreditation of Counseling and Related Educational Programs (CACREP)

An independent agency recognized by the Council for Higher Education Accreditation to accredit counseling and related educational programs whose aim is promote excellence in professional preparation in a number of fields including school counseling.

criminal action

A court action brought by the state against an individual charged with an offense against the state. Such actions may result in a fine or incarceration of the defendant.

criminal court

A court that hears criminal cases.

criminal law

The body of the law dealing with crime and punishment and the obligation of citizens to obey laws intended to protect society. It involves a legal action filed by a state or by the United States against a particular individual or individuals.

criminal negligence

Reckless disregard for the safety of others. It is the willful indifference to an injury that could follow an act. Reckless disregard of a professional duty based in law that results in harm to another. An example is the failure of a mental health professional to report child abuse, which leads to the further abuse and harm to the child.

critical-evaluative level

A level of reasoning that involves three hierarchically arranged stages or tiers of examination to resolve a moral dilemma; involves the evaluation of the implications of laws, ethical principles, and ethical theories bearing on the ethical decision to be made.

cross-cultural counseling

Cf. *multicultural counseling.*

cross-examination

The questioning by the opposing attorney of a witness for the other side, after the witness has testified. The attorney is allowed to challenge the witness's testimony by asking leading questions and seeking inconsistencies.

cruel and unusual punishment
Punishment deemed to be offensive to an ordinary individual. Such punishment is forbidden by law.

cultural encapsulation
A tendency to treat clients and others from the practitioner's own cultural perspective without regard to cultural differences.

cultural sensitivity
The capability to recognize and appreciate differences in cultural values, mores, and practices in individuals and groups of different backgrounds and cultures.

culturally disadvantaged
A term utilized by some counseling personnel to describe some aspect of a multicultural group.

culture
The constellation of shared values, beliefs, stories, customs, and rules that characterize an organization or community. It is to an organization or community what personality is to an individual.

custodial parent
The divorced parent with whom the children live and who is typically the recipient of child support.

custody
Refers to the rights and responsibilities of parents with regard to their children. Legal custody involves the right and responsibility of the parent to make decisions about the child's life, whereas physical custody is the right and responsibility of the parent to reside with the child, and provide for his/her immediate well-being (clothes, shelter, food).

custody dispute
A disagreement between parents over the rights to their children.

custody evaluation
An examination of children's home environment and their relationships with their parents used by a court in awarding custody. Evaluators are typically court-appointed mental health professionals who undertake such evaluations.

cybercounseling
Professional counseling that occurs on the Internet. A controversial method of treatment because of issues involving the therapeutic relationship and confidentiality. Also called cybertherapy and Internet counseling.

damages
Compensation claimed by the plaintiff or ordered by the courts for injuries sustained by the plaintiff that resulted from the wrongful actions of the defendant.

danger to self or others
A designation indicating suicidal or aggressive threats or actions. Legal test used to determine if an individual should be involuntarily confined and whether confidentiality can be breached.

dangerous client
A client determined or deemed to be a danger to self, the practitioner, or others. Practitioners have a duty to breach confidentiality with such clients and warn and/or protect foreseeable victims or individuals.

date rape
Rape by a dating partner wherein the rapist typically perceives sex as consensual and the victim's resistance as game playing.

Daubert test
A modern legal test for the admissibility of scientific evidence based on the U.S. Supreme Court case of *Daubert v. Merrell Dow Pharmaceuticals*. Decided in 1994, this test requires that proposed scientific evidence be developed by use of the scientific method and be helpful to the court.

More lenient than the previously accepted *Frye* test and accepted by all federal and many state courts. Cf. *Frye test.*

de facto
Literally means "in fact," and refers to a situation or community practice that exists in fact irrespective of whether it is lawful. Its legal complement is *de jure.*

de jure
Literally means "by right or law" and refers to state or affair sanctioned by a civil authority and has the force of law behind it.

decision
A court's conclusion or judgment in contrast to the reasoning or opinion of the court.

decree
A court order issued in an equity suit.

defamation injury
Harm done to an individual's character or reputation as a result of the false statements of another made to a third party. Defamation is called "libel" when the false statement is written, and "slander" when it is spoken. Practitioners should note that an erroneous diagnosis can be the basis for a defamation suit against the practitioner.

defendant
In a criminal case, it is the individual accused of committing a crime, whereas in a civil suit, it is the individual against whom the suit is brought.

deinstitutionalization
The release of individuals from a mental institution usually by the order of a court or a civil authority.

deontological ethics
Cf. *duty ethics.*

dependent child
A child who is a ward of the courts or a child owed support by a parent or parents.

deposition
A type of pretrial discovery consisting of statements by a witness under oath in a question-and-answer format as in a court of law with the

opportunity for cross-examination. Such statements may be admitted into evidence if it is impossible for a witness to attend a trial in person.

determinism
Ethical perspective wherein all human behavior is the necessary and inevitable result of prior causes. The opposite of free will.

developmentally disabled
A condition marked by subnormal abilities that is similar to mental retardation or developmentally delayed but usually involves selective deficits.

differential diagnosis
The process of describing a client wherein the diagnosis of one psychiatric disorder is considered more appropriate than another disorder or disorders with similar diagnostic signs and symptoms.

dignity
The inherent, unalterable value and respect due every individual by virtue of being human.

dimensional boundaries
The view that although professional relationships involve power differentials, relationships are not inherently abusive or exploitive. Even though boundaries are useful and necessary in professional relationships, they can be discussed openly by mental health professional and client, and boundary crossings, when appropriate, can facilitate the therapeutic relationship and treatment outcomes.

diminished capacity
A state of mental functionality that falls below a normal standard, which may disqualify an individual from giving a legal testimony or bearing a legal responsibility.

diplomate
The term used by some health care professions such as medicine and psychology to designate the attainment of specialty credentials within a specific area of advanced practice. Also referred to as "board certified." Cf. *certification*.

direct liability
Liability that occurs when the harm that is done by the supervisee is a result of the supervision itself.

direct-examination
The questioning of a witness in court by the attorney that called that witness to testify and that is, typically, followed by a cross-examination by the attorney representing the other side.

disability
An identifiable physical or mental condition whose functional limitations, when manifested, are recognized and may be overcome with appropriate accommodations. Cf. *Americans with Disability Act (ADA)*.

discovery
A pretrial evidence-gathering process that includes testimony and documents for the purpose of ascertaining facts of a case not already admitted.

discretion
Involves choices made within professional parameters in which practitioners may exercise flexibility to act as they think best. In clinical settings, may be applied to a practitioner-employee's freedom to act in a client's best interest, or flexibility to make decisions regarding care.

dismissal
A final disposition of a suit by a court without hearing, or full hearing, of the complaint.

dissociative amnesia
Inability to recall important personal information, usually of a traumatic or stressful nature, that is too extensive to be explained by ordinary forgetfulness. In this state, clients generally present with a retrospectively reported gap or series of gaps in memory for certain aspects of that client's history. They often have histories of "forgotten" early childhood traumas.

dissolution of marriage
The name for divorce in some no-fault states such as California.

distance learning
The use of technical equipment or media instead of live teachers for the delivery of training or education.

diversion
Individual counseling, group counseling, or similar intervention that is offered as an alternative to incarceration. For example, a first offender convicted of driving under the influence (DUI) of alcohol is referred for group therapy.

divorce
The legal ending or dissolution of a marriage.

divorce mediation
A negotiation or conflict resolution process by which a mediator helps a divorcing couple to develop and agree to a written divorce agreement. Required of divorcing couples in some states.

domestic violence
Violence occurring within family relationships as well as between individuals who are in a romantic relationship or who have lived together.

do-not-resuscitate
Directive of a physician to withhold lifesaving measures in the event a patient experiences cardiac or respiratory arrest. For such an order to be legal, it must be obtained from the patient or family or legal advocate, be in writing, signed, and dated by a physician. Abbreviated as DNR.

downcoding
Giving a client a less serious or severe diagnosis to obtain treatment.

dual relationship
A professional counseling or supervisory relationship that occurs alongside or simultaneously with a personal and nonprofessional relationship with the same individual. These relationships can be conflicting (boundary violations) or complimentary (boundary crossings). When a relationship involves more than two roles it is referred to as a multiple relationship. Cf. *boundary violations* and *boundary crossings*.

due care (professional)
A standard of care or duty owed to a client. Professionals whose practice is below that standard can be held legally liable if negligence is proved.

due process
The right of an individual to be given notice of adverse actions and to a process that allows a defense against the action.

due process in supervision
A sequence of procedures that a supervisor must observe in providing a supervisee with reasonable notice of the intent to provide a negative evaluation or recommendation.

31

durable power of attorney
A legal instrument authorizing a designated individual to act on another's behalf. In a health care setting, it includes the authority to make treatment decisions for another.

Durham test
A rule for determining criminal responsibility in individuals with mental disease or defect for the purpose of establishing an insanity defense. Few, if any, courts use this test.

duty
An obligation or legal responsibility that arises out of a contract or operation of law and that is owed by one individual or entity to another. It requires a practitioner to take or refrain from action, perform in a certain fashion, or maintain a standard of care. A breach of a duty under a contract or operation of law may subject the practitioner to civil liability under contract or tort law such as a malpractice suit for negligent injury.

duty ethics
The ethical theory that considers the intention of the person choosing, the means, and the nature of the act itself. An act is considered morally good and right if it is done for the sake of duty, has a good motive, its means are acceptable, and/or the nature of the act itself is good.

duty to predict
A duty based on the special relationship of a practitioner and client that requires the practitioner to judge the probability that the client is a danger to self or others.

duty to prevent harm
A duty based on the special relationship of a practitioner and client that requires the practitioner to take steps to prevent a client from committing suicide or other injury to self or others.

duty to protect
A duty based on the special relationship of a practitioner and client that requires the practitioner to protect the intended victims of a dangerous client. A broader duty than the duty to warn. Creates an exception to the general rule of confidentiality and imposes a legal obligation on practitioners to contact and warn the intended victim when a client states in therapy an intent to harm a specific victim but also requires the practitioner to take prompt, proactive measures to safeguard the intended victim,

such as involving law enforcement. Some consider this duty to apply to clients with suicidal intent as well.

duty to report
A duty to report abuse or suspected abuse of children, the elderly, and in some states, the disabled, in a timely manner. Typically, practitioners are expected to meet this duty although different jurisdictions specify other professionals who are also required to meet it. Also called mandatory reporting.

duty to warn
A duty or legal responsibility based on the special relationship of a practitioner and client to inform an endangered party or parties when it is believed that a client poses a serious danger to them. Generally creates an exception to the rule of confidentiality. Often referred to as the Tarasoff duty.

emancipation
The process by which a minor achieves legal adult status.

employee-employer relationship
Nature and extent of the work relationship between employee and employer. In determining whether an employee-employer relationship existed, courts will look to a multitude of factors, such as whether the employer, which in most cases will be an agency or university, had control over the firing and hiring of the supervisee, or whether the agency or university had any power to control the supervisee's conduct. The actual exchange of remuneration for services, although one of the factors the court may consider, is not necessary to establish an employee-employer relationship.

enterprise liability
Legal theory wherein supervisor liability is involved when it is determined the supervisee's acts or behavior were a foreseeable risk. Applicable for supervisors who charge clients for their supervisee's services, potentially generating a profit. Accordingly, the benefits derived by the supervisor from the revenues generated from the supervisee's services are balanced by the risk of having to compensate an injured client.

Equal Employment Opportunity Commission
A government agency enacted by Congress to administer the employment aspects of the Civil Rights Act of 1964. It forbids discrimination in the workplace.

equal protection of the law
A guarantee that no individual is denied the same protection of the laws that is enjoyed by other individuals in similar circumstances. Such denial is prohibited by the 14th Amendment.

equity law
A branch of law primarily concerned with providing justice and fair treatment. It addresses issues the common law is unable to consider.

ethic of being
Basic orientation to ethical and moral reasoning that assumes that ethics should primarily be oriented toward the development of what an individual ought to be rather than about the question of the rightness or wrongness of specific actions. It emphasizes character and virtue. Virtue ethics, care ethics, and narrative ethics are prominent approaches to being ethics.

ethic of care
Cf. *care ethics.*

ethic of doing
Basic orientation to ethical and moral reasoning, which assumes that ethics should primarily be oriented toward the moral status of specific actions, rather than on what an individual should be, that is, virtue and character. Consequentialist ethics, rights ethical, and duty ethics, that is, deontological ethics, are prominent approaches to doing ethics.

ethical absolutism
Ethical principle that binds all individuals in all situations without exception. It is based on the premise that one or more ethical absolutes exists and can be discovered.

ethical anxiety
Feeling of despair triggered by the necessity to make ethical and moral decisions. Considered to be a necessary attribute in the formation of moral character.

ethical climate
The dimension of organizational culture that reflects the shared perceptions that staff and colleagues hold concerning ethical procedures and practices occurring with an organization.

ethical dilemma
Conflicts that arise when competing standards of right and wrong apply to a specific situation in counseling practice. They arise because of competing or conflicting ethical standards, because of a conflict between an ethical and moral standard, because specific ethical standards do not address complex situations, or because other factors prevent a clear-cut application of the standard.

ethical principles
Higher-level norms or directives within a society that are consistent with its moral principles and that constitute higher standards of moral behavior or attitudes. They build on and give meaning and direction to one or more ethical values.

ethical sensitivity
The capacity to recognize situations and circumstances that have implications for the welfare or well-being of another. Ethical awareness is a prerequisite for ethical sensitivity.

ethical theories
Broad perspectives that provide an orientation to ethical situations and are the way one chooses to live out and interpret one's values. Major ethical theories include consequentialist ethics, rights ethics, duty ethics, virtue ethics, care ethics, and narrative ethics.

ethical values
Beliefs, attitudes, or moral goods that are useful guides in everyday living. They are single words that identify something as being desirable for human beings. Common ethical values in counseling and psychotherapy are beneficence, nonmaleficence, fidelity, autonomy or responsibility, justice, fidelity, compassion, integrity, and respect for persons.

ethical violation
An action that violates the letter or the spirit of an ethical standard of practice.

ethical virtues
Ethical values that are routinely practiced and incorporated into one's basic character.

ethics
The science of how choices are made or should be made. This contrasts with morality, which is the activity of making choices and of deciding, judging, justifying, and defending those actions or behaviors called moral. Thus, ethics is the study of morality. In short, it is the philosophical study of moral behavior, of moral decision making, or how one leads a good life.

ethics–aspirational
Ethical values and principles that greatly exceed minimal, prescribed ethical values and principles, which are referred to as mandatory ethics.

ethics–mandatory
The minimum level of ethical guidance focusing on compliance with laws and standards of a professional code of ethics, and that is not optional for the practice of that profession. Also referred to as mandatory ethics. The opposite of aspirational ethics.

ethics–philosophical
A branch of philosophy concerning theories of what is "good," "right," or "worthy." In contrast to applied ethics, which is specific and pragmatic, philosophical ethics is theoretical.

ethics–professional
Agreed-on rules or standards established by a profession that define what is acceptable or "good" practice.

ethics audit
An audit or investigation in which the implementation of ethical policies as well as ethical incidents in an organizational setting are reviewed and evaluated.

ethics of care
An ethical theory and approach that emphasizes human connectedness, or a relational perspective.

ethnicity
Property of individuals who share a common origin and a unique social and cultural heritage.

eudaemonism
Ethical principle in which happiness is considered the highest good and the basis of moral obligation. Aristotle was one of the first to propose such an ethics of happiness. Cf. *Aristotle.*

euthanasia
The intentional termination of life. The word is derived from the Greek meaning "good death" and has come to mean death with dignity of the hopelessly ill, injured, or incapacitated. Also referred to as assisted suicide or mercy killing.

evidence
That which is presented as proof in support of a claim made in a legal proceeding.

exception
An exemption from a law defining situations in which the original laws do not apply. For instance, whereas client-practitioner communications are normally confidential and protected, disclosures regarding abuse of a child or the elderly are exceptions and must be reported. (Clients must be forewarned of this exception.)

existentialist ethics
Approach to ethics that contends that ethics should begin with the subjective, that is, personal meaning and choice, which is the basis for knowing rather than with the objective, that is, absolute ethical categories.

expert testimony
The sworn testimony and opinion of an expert given to help a judge and/or jury in the deliberation and determination of truth.

expert witness
An individual designated as an expert based on special training, experience, skill, and/or knowledge in a relevant area who is allowed to offer an opinion as testimony in court or a legal proceeding.

exploitation
Acts or behavior that take unjust advantage of another for one's own benefit. May be sexual or monetary, such as when caretakers require elderly individuals they are caring for to purchase expensive gifts for them as a condition of continued care.

eyewitness
An individual who reports having observed or witnessed some event or thing.

failure to commit
A negligent act by a mental health professional who fails to initiate or institute involuntary confinement on a client who is deemed to be dangerous to self or others.

fair evaluation in supervision
The duty to insure that a supervisor evaluates a supervisee in a manner that is fair, consistent, and equitable, and that provides a way to remediate identified problems and skill deficits.

fair preponderance of the evidence
A low burden of proof used only in civil law suits. It represents a "more-likely-than-not burden of proof" of at least 51% of needed evidence.

false imprisonment
The intentional action of wrongfully confining another without his or her consent. Such confinement by force or intimidation denies the individual the liberty to move freely.

false memory
A memory of an event that did not happen, or a memory of the distortion of an event that did occur. Believed to be a memory implanted by suggestion or some other source of subsequent information that did not originate in a real event. This is a very controversial concept in sexual abuse cases.

Family Educational Rights and Privacy Act
Federal law since 1974 regarding parental right to review student records, determining who may access records, determining what information can be disclosed from a student record without consent, and providing guidelines for counselors' "personal notes." Applies to all schools and districts that receive federal funds. Also known as FERPA and the Buckley Amendment.

family law
A branch of civil law involving marriage, divorce, adoption, and related areas.

father absence syndrome
The constellation of harmful effects due to the absence of a father during the course of a child's development. Common symptoms include guilt, depression, and anger, although it may differ for boys and girls.

father custody
Custody of children awarded by a court to the father after separation or divorce.

fees
The amount of money charged for a certain time period spent with the practitioner, or, in some cases, for a particular service performed by the practitioner, such as an evaluation.

felony
Serious crime that typically leads to imprisonment for a period longer than one year, or to death, in some jurisdictions.

feminist ethics
Approach to ethics based on feminism and that begins with women's experience as the situation out of which ethical understanding arises. It challenges inequalities at every level of society and life. Care ethics is one form of it.

FERPA
Cf. *Family Educational Rights and Privacy Act.*

fidelity
The ethical virtue and principle that directs individuals to keep commitments or promises.

fiduciary
The entity that has the duty to act in a trustworthy manner and to keep safe and sound that which belongs to another. A relationship between individuals in which each is expected to act out of a position of trust for another. Mental health practitioners have a fiduciary responsibility for their clients.

finding
The conclusion reached by a court or jury regarding a question of fact or law.

foreseeability
A legal test for liability in which a practitioner must attempt to foresee and prevent injury. Failure to do so is considered negligence.

foster care
Program providing care and shelter for displaced and homeless children as well as for certain disabled adults.

free will
Ability to choose and act on the basis of rational choice. The opposite of determinism. Moral actions are assumed to originate from will or volition rather than as random events. Cf. *determinism.*

Frye test
The test of admissibility of scientific testimony and procedures based on *Frye v. United States* in which the court declared that acceptance by the scientific community is essential before such evidence is accepted in the legal community.

general ethics
Branch of philosophy that studies the basic nature of morality. Synonymous with philosophical ethics and analytical ethics.

good and goodness
Good means morally excellent, whereas goodness refers to the quality or state of being good.

"good faith" mandatory report
Report made by the practitioner without malice, based on professional counseling judgment.

good life
The ultimate goal or value that an individual strives to achieve. Ethically, it is foundational to morality and ethical decision making in that individuals order their lives in accord with their ultimate value.

good Samaritan laws
Laws designed to protect those—usually health care professionals—who render aid in an emergency, and that provide limited immunity for such individuals from any civil suit arising out of care rendered provided it was not done in a grossly negligent manner. In some jurisdictions, such laws oblige witnesses to provide help to those in need.

grand jury
A specially convened jury that determines whether there is sufficient evidence that a crime has been committed to justify bringing a case to trial.

grandparent visitation
The right of grandparents to visit their grandchildren.

guardian
Person appointed by a court to protect the interests of and make decisions for a person who is incapable of making his or her own decisions.

guardian ad litem
Literally means "guardian for the litigation." A legal representative, usually an attorney, appointed by a judge to represent the interests of an individual who is a minor or is legally incompetent.

habit

Learned behavior pattern that is performed automatically. There is moral overtone in that habits can be either good or bad. In virtue ethics theory, it is believed that the formation of virtue, that is, good habits, is an individual's chief ethical task in life. Cf. *virtue*.

handicap

Inability to participate freely in activities typical to an individual's age and gender due to a physical or mental abnormality. By contrast, "disability" is a permanent impairment that may not be a handicap depending on the degree and coping capacity. Cf. *disability*.

happiness

A state of contentment, in ethics refers to living well. According to Aristotle, it cannot be obtained directly but is the by-product of the pursuit of excellence, virtue, and rational action in a life that affords the opportunity for them.

hastened death

Refers to the decision of a terminally ill individual who voluntarily stops eating and drinking, terminates life support when dependent on it, or refuses aggressive treatment designed to stop the progression of an illness.

health care proxy
Document delegating the authority to another individual—known as a proxy or health care agent—to make one's own health care decisions in the event one is incapacitated or otherwise unable to make his/her own decisions.

Health Insurance Portability and Accountability Act
The federal law designed to protect clients' privacy related to their medical information. It standardizes procedures across the United States for insuring the privacy and confidentiality of protected health information, including counseling and psychotherapy information. Often designated as HIPAA.

health maintenance organization
A type of managed care organization usually abbreviated as HMO.

hearing
An oral proceeding before a trial court to ascertain facts and provide evidence. Distinguished from "arguments," which are oral proceedings before an appellate court for presentation of ideas.

Helsinki Declaration
Declaration by the World Medical Association advocating full informed consent for any biomedical research, particularly when children or incompetent individuals are research subjects. Unlike the Belmont Report, this declaration did not cover behavioral research.

high suggestibility
A theory positing that the effects of hypnosis are largely the result of enhanced suggestibility. Some professionals believe that hypnosis can be a tool for implanting false memory in individuals with high suggestibility.

HIPAA
Cf. *Health Insurance Portability and Accountability Act.*

HMO
Cf. *health maintenance organization.*

holder of privilege
The individual legally empowered to waive or assert a legal privilege against disclosure. Because privilege is the prerogative of the holder, it is important that practitioners recognize that the holder of client-practitioner privilege is the client.

hospice
Medical programs for terminally ill individuals with a psychosocial and spiritual orientation. Emphasizes palliative rather than curative treatment and can provide clients care in their own home. It neither hastens nor prolongs death but, rather, supports pain reduction and death with dignity.

hospital privileges
The right of a professional to admit and/or treat patients in a hospital or provide services in or through an agency or institution.

human nature
Psychological, social, and philosophical qualities that characterize what it means to be human.

human subjects committee
A formally designated committee that reviews proposed research studies using human subjects or participants for the purpose of preventing ethical and legal violations. Cf. *institutional review board*.

humanism
Philosophical perspective that emphasizes the primary importance, value, and dignity of human beings. Various forms include Christian and secular humanism, which are often contrasted. For example, secular humanism rejects revelation and the supernatural in favor of rational thinking and the cultural accomplishments of humans.

idealism
Philosophical theory asserting that reality is ultimately mental and spiritual rather than material and physical. Ethical approaches based on this theory identify moral obligation with duty, categorical imperative, or absolute spirit.

immoral
Conduct that transgresses moral prohibitions, violates moral sensitivities, or conflicts with moral principles.

impairment
The incapacity to perform specific functions because of a debilitating medical, substance-related, or psychological condition that results in diminished functioning from a previous higher level of functioning.

impeach
Efforts to demonstrate that the testimony and a witness are not credible.

impeachment of experts
Effort by an opposing lawyer to discredit an expert called to testify in a case.

in loco parentis
Latin term meaning "in place of the parent." A legal doctrine that assigns a parent's rights, duties, and responsibilities to others, for example, school administration or a court.

incompetence
The incapacity to perform the function of the practitioner role because of insufficient training or experience, unwillingness, or inflexibility. Important to distinguish from impairment. Cf. *impairment*.

incompetency
Legal term referring to the condition of an individual, such as a client, who has been legally declared to be incapable of exercising some civil right or privilege, in which case he or she is not held responsible for his or her acts.

independence
Being free to make one's own decisions and to act autonomously.

independent living
Movement of the early 1990s to emphasize the living needs of persons with disabilities.

indeterminate confinement
Holding someone in a locked psychiatric unit or institution with no specified time for release. In most jurisdictions, such confinement is not legal unless the result of a judicial proceeding.

indictment
Formal written accusation presented by a grand jury or a judge, which charges an individual with criminal conduct.

indirect services
Services provided wherein a practitioner does not engage in direct communication with a client, and in which there is no intent to provide counseling services directly to that individual.

informed consent
Legal concept wherein a client has the right to know the potential risks, benefits, and alternatives of a proposed treatment or services prior to undergoing it.

informed consent to treatment
The client's right to decide whether to participate in treatment after the practitioner fully describes the services to be rendered in a manner that is understandable by the client.

injunction
A court order prohibiting a person from committing an act that threatens or may result in injury to the plaintiff or to another.

inpatient
The status of being treated in a residential setting such as a mental hospital. Practitioners have more duties to control inpatients. The opposite is outpatient—a status that allows a client to go home after receiving treatment from a facility.

insanity
A legal status designating that a defendant cannot be held responsible for his or her criminal behavior. Distinguished from serious mental illness. Cf. *insanity defense*.

insanity defense
Defense that contends that a defendant's criminal action is a result of insanity. There are four types of insanity defense: Durham test, model penal code test, M'Naghten test, and irresistible impulse test.

institutional review board
A human subjects committee that services an entire institution. Such committees are federally mandated for any organization whose research is federally funded and must include a diverse membership including a community representative. Abbreviated as IRB.

institutional
Confining an individual within a mental institution. Called "involuntary confinement" when against the individual's will.

integrity
The ethical value and principle that involves promoting accuracy, honesty, and truthfulness while striving to keep one's promises and to avoid unwise or unclear commitments.

intent
A state of mind in which the individual knows and desires the consequences of his/her act. Typically, proving intent to harm or damage is not necessary for civil findings of negligence.

intention
Motive dictating a specific action. In criminal cases, it is viewed as pivotal in determining the guilt of the accused.

interrogatory
Method of discovery for gathering relevant information whereby attorneys either issue a subpoena or request that the court issue a subpoena that requires the individual being served to provide an answer or answers to a written question or questions under oath.

intuitive level
A level of reasoning that reflects the influence of the practitioner's everyday personal and professional moral wisdom in the process of ethical decision making.

involuntary commitment
Procedure whereby an individual who is at risk for harming himself or another can be involuntarily confined for a designated period of time during which a psychiatric evaluation will be conducted. Cf. *involuntary confinement*.

involuntary confinement
Confining individuals to a mental institution without their consent. Without clinical justification and due process, it may constitute false imprisonment.

irreconcilable differences
Differences that cannot be mended in a marriage. In many states, it is grounds for a no-fault divorce.

irresistible impulse test
A defense of insanity in which it is demonstrated that the defendant had a mental disease and that his or her action is an irresistible result of his or her mental disease.

Jaffee v. Redmond

The case by which the U.S. Supreme Court established a practitioner-patient privilege under federal common law. The Court held that "confidential communications between a licensed psychotherapist and her patients in the course of diagnosis or treatment are protected from compelled disclosure under Rule 501 of the Federal Rules of Evidence." Cf. *psychotherapist-client privileged communication*.

joint custody

A custody arrangement wherein each parent is allowed significant time with the child or children and each parent shares in significant decisions. Also known as shared custody. Cf. *joint legal custody* and *joint physical custody*.

joint legal custody

Custody agreement in which parents share rights to make major decisions about a child's life and well-being, including medical, religious, and educational decisions.

joint physical custody

Custody agreement in which each parent has significant time living with the child.

judgment

Decision rendered by a court.

jurisdiction
A court's authority to hear cases; the geopolitical area in which a court has the right and authorization to function.

jury
Individuals selected and sworn in to hear the evidence, determine the facts in a case, and render a verdict.

justice
The ethical virtue and principle that fosters fairness and equity and provides equal treatment to all individuals.

knew-or-should-have-known doctrine
The legal test for determining responsibility for knowing something.

law
Basic rules of order of a society, which are legislated or codified by a government. Statutory law refers to laws passed by legislatures, whereas case law refers to law derived from court decisions.

law of evidence
The law specifying which types of evidence can be admitted during legal proceedings and the conditions for admissibility.

lay witness
A witness who is not an expert witness. The scope of the testimony of lay witness is usually more restricted than for experts.

layered supervision
The type of supervision in which doctoral students supervise master's students who are themselves being supervised by faculty.

leadership
The process of visioning and exercising responsibility, power, and authority over others, with their recognition and acceptance of such influence.

leading question
A question asked by a lawyer at trial or deposition that suggests to the witness the answer that he or she should give. Leading questions are allowed

when the witness is one who is defined as "hostile" or an adverse witness. Leading questions are used during cross-examination.

least restrictive alternative
The legal doctrine requiring the least confining or least harmful treatment or placement. Treatment provided in the least restrictive setting is preferred over that in more restrictive settings. For example, outpatient treatment is considered less restrictive than inpatient treatment.

legal duty
A duty imposed by case law or statute. If an individual having the duty breaches it, he/she can be held liable for damages.

legal guardian
An individual appointed by a court to make decisions regarding the overall welfare of another, including their property.

legal representative
An adult authorized by a court to make legal decisions for a minor or an incompetent adult. Cf. *guardian ad litem*.

legalism
Ethical perspective that identifies morality with strict observance of law or adherence to moral codes.

liability
An obligation incurred through a negligent act.

liability insurance
Contract in which a client can be compensated for the harm that results from a practitioner's negligence in return for premium payments by a practitioner.

libel
False or malicious writing intended to defame or dishonor another and that is published such that others will observe it.

licensing board
A government or paragovernmental agency empowered to regulate both the issuance of professional licenses as well as the conduct of professionals having such a license.

licensing exam
An examination given or approved by a licensing board that must be passed to obtain a license.

licensing statute
A law that specifies the requirements for professional licensing and that regulates the conduct of individuals licensed under it.

licensure
A form of professional regulation that restricts both the use of a professional title, such as "psychologist," and the practice of the profession.

limits of practice
The boundaries that demarcate the acceptable activities associated with a profession.

litigation
A lawsuit or formal contesting of a dispute in a court. The opposite of negotiation.

living will
Document of specific directives regarding medical procedures that should or should not be provided in specific circumstances. The individual expresses these directives in advance in the event that he/she becomes incapacitated at a future time.

malfeasance
Commission of an unlawful or improper act.

malicious prosecution
A legal cause of action against a defendant alleging that a case filed by a defendant against plaintiff was based primarily on personal animosity.

malpractice
Violation of a professional duty expected of a reasonably prudent practitioner and involves performing below the professional standard of care. It is a form of negligence that requires four specific elements to be met. Thus, to prove a case of negligence, the plaintiff must show that at the time of the alleged negligent incident, (a) a legal duty between the practitioner and the client existed, (b) the practitioner breached that duty, (c) and that the client suffered harm or injury, (d) which was directly and proximately caused by the practitioner's breach of duty.

managed behavioral health care organization
An organization that administrates and oversees the delivery of behavioral or mental health services with the expectation of improving quality of care and cost containment. Abbreviated as MBHCO.

managed care
Provision of health care services, including counseling and psychother-apy, through medical insurance managed or overseen by a managed care organization that serves as a mediator between insurance carriers and health care professionals.

managed care contract
An agreement between a managed care organization and a practitioner-provider defining the types of services to be provided, the maximum fee, and limitations of services.

managed care organization
An organization that administrates and oversees the delivery of health services with the expectation of improving quality of care and cost con-tainment. Abbreviated as MCO. Also referred to as a health maintenance organization (HMO).

mandatory ethics
The most basic level of ethical guidance focusing on compliance with laws and standards of a professional code of ethics, and that are not optional for the practice of that profession.

mandatory reporting
Act required of a designated professional to report known or suspected vulnerable groups from physical and sexual abuse and exploitation in a timely manner. Cf. *mandatory reporting law*.

mandatory reporting law
A law requiring certain professionals to report abuse and neglect to a des-ignated government agency. Such laws take precedence over laws protect-ing confidentiality, and thus practitioners are required to report credible evidence of child abuse.

marital communications privilege
The right of one partner to forbid the other partner from testifying against him/her in legal proceedings. In many jurisdictions, private communica-tion between partners during marriage is considered privileged. At the option of a witness partner, and in some states either partner can prevent the other from testifying about such communication even after divorce.

marital property
Property belonging to a couple that is divided in the event of a divorce. Called community property in a community property state.

marital rape
Forced sexual intercourse in a marriage relationship.

marital settlement agreement
An agreement between divorcing parties that settles one or more of the issues that otherwise would be litigated and decided by judicial order after a trial.

mediation
An alternative dispute resolution process in which a mediator helps both parties to arrive at an acceptable solution. Typically, divorce mediation is a private mediation of the terms of divorce by an attorney and one or more mental health professionals.

Medicaid
A state-administered program for the medically indigent.

Medicare
An American health insurance program administered by the Social Security Administration for individuals 65 or older and for disabled individuals eligible for benefits.

membership
The status of being a member of a professional organization. Usually voluntary, with specific education and/or experience requirements and the expectation of following the organization's code of ethics.

mental health law
Laws governing the confinement and treatment of mentally ill and mentally retarded or developmentally disabled individuals. It is characterized by a blend of criminal lawlike protections with an intermediate burden or standard of proof.

mental health professionals
Professionals who work in the fields of counseling, psychology, psychiatry, marital and family therapy, and social work.

mental retardation
Denotes subnormal intelligence and adaptive abilities often reflected by global deficits in behavior, cognition, and affect. Also referred to as developmental disability.

mental status examination
A structured interview process that provides a controlled interpersonal setting in which to observe and elicit the symptoms and signs of possible mental disorders, as well as cognitive and perceptual functioning or deficits and levels of judgment and insight.

Miranda warning
A warning that police are required to give when an investigation turns accusatorial. Defendants must be apprised of the adverse legal consequences of giving a confession or statement and informed of their right to an attorney. Cf. *psychological Miranda warning.*

misdemeanor
An intermediate-level crime, more serious than an infraction (a parking ticket) and less serious than a felony (murder). Normally penalties for being found guilty of a misdemeanor are limited to fines and less than one year in jail.

misfeasance
A type of malpractice involving improper performance of a duty. Cf. *malfeasance.*

misrepresentation
Intentional deception that misleads and causes harm.

mistrial
A trial stopped by the judge and declared void before a verdict is rendered. It indicates a failure of the trial process, a failure to achieve a judgment for either party.

M'Naghten test
A type of insanity defense in which it must be clearly demonstrated that because of his/her mental disease or defect, a defendant was incapable of understanding the difference between right and wrong and forming the intent or mind set required by the crime.

moral development
The gradual development of an individual's conception of right and wrong, ethical and religious values, conscience, and moral behavior. The cognitive-structural approach described by Kohlberg posits that moral norms are embedded within the primary and universal structures of social relations and that justice is the most basic norm.

morality
Activity of making choices and of deciding, judging, justifying, and defending those actions or behaviors called moral. This contrasts with ethics, which is the body of principles that studies how choices were made or should be made. Thus, ethics is the study of morality.

morals
The principles that inform and guide an individual. Sometimes these principles derive from a religious standard. Can be called moral principles.

motion
A request that a judge take a certain action such as dismissing a case.

multicultural counseling
A helping relationship involving two or more individuals with different socially constructed worldviews.

multiculturalism
Acceptance of racial, ethnic, religious, linguistic, and socially constructed worldviews.

narrative ethics
The ethical theory that insists that narrative or story and its context are important in ethical decision making. An act is considered morally good and right if it reflects the ongoing story of an individual's life, culture, and tradition within which he or she lives it.

National Career Development Association (NCDA)
The professional association representing and advocating for career counseling.

National Model for School Counseling Programs
Model based on national standards developed for the school counseling profession in 1997. A competency-based model that addresses the academic, career, and personal/social needs of students while providing direction for the delivery, management, and accountability of a comprehensive developmental program.

National Standards for School Counseling Programs
Research-based standards directing the vision and goals of school counseling, which provide the structure for a systematic, collaborative, and comprehensive model for school counselors to use as they integrate developmental goals addressing the academic, personal/social, and career needs of students into the school curriculum.

natural law
Philosophical concept wherein law is believed to exist in nature and can be discovered by a reasonable individual. Also, a norm for ethical behavior, which is derived from nature, right reason, or religion, and believed to be binding on all humans. To the extent it can be known by reason alone, it provides guidance for all individuals and when followed enhances the common good.

natural supports
A term that emphasizes using individuals and things that are naturally occurring within the individual's environment as reasonable accommodations for those with disabilities.

neglect
Failure to provide necessary food, care, clothing, supervision, emotional support or medical attention for a child, the disabled, and the elderly.

negligence
Dereliction of a duty that directly causes damage to a client. It is the omission or commission of an act that a reasonable prudent practitioner would or would not do under given circumstances, and a form of carelessness that constitutes a departure from the standard of care expected of mental health professionals.

negligent hiring
Legal theory wherein liability is established on the basis of whether the university or employer had prior knowledge of an employee's or student's history of dangerousness. Accordingly, if a university has knowledge that a student has a documented history of dangerous behavior and the university places that student at an agency site without disclosing the student's proclivity toward dangerousness, the university may be held liable for negligent hiring. Conversely, if the agency fails to ask whether the student has a history of dangerous behavior prior to accepting that student for placement, the agency may be held liable for negligent hiring. In essence, in negligent hiring, liability is established on the basis of whether the university or employer had prior knowledge of the student's dangerous history or failed to establish his or her integrity and character.

negligent supervision
Negligence of a supervisor. In order to prove negligent supervision, a plaintiff client must show that the supervisor failed to use ordinary care

in supervision by failing to prevent the supervisee's foreseeable misconduct and that there was a direct link between the supervisor's acts of commission or omission and the resultant injury to the client.

negotiation
Process of discussion and debate of an issue in which at least two individuals attempt to achieve some agreement.

No Child Left Behind Act
Federal legislation that requires increased accountability for student achievement outcomes. Schools must demonstrate progress toward academic goals for all students as measured by standardized tests. Also known as Public Law 107–110.

no fault divorce
Refers to grounds for divorce based on relationship incompatibilities, that is, irreconcilable differences, instead of the wrongdoing of a partner. Advocates the avoidance of fault finding in order to reduce prolonged litigation and the bitterness of divorce.

noncustodial parent
The divorced parent who has only visitation rights to see his/her child or children. This parent may have the obligation to pay child support.

nonfeasance
The omission or failure to act or perform a duty in a manner required of a reasonably prudent individual in similar circumstances. Can be a form of malpractice for a practitioner.

nonmaleficence
The ethical value and principle requiring that individuals refrain from any action that might cause harm to another.

norm
Rule, law, or principle that prescribes, governs, and directs some aspects of ethical conduct. It is a standard for evaluating character or moral behavior.

not guilty by reason of insanity
Legal finding that a defendant, that is, an individual accused of committing a criminal act, should not be held responsible for the crime because the defendant was found to be legally insane at the time the criminal act was committed.

objection
Attempt by an attorney to prevent evidence from being admitted during a legal proceeding on the basis that the evidence does not fit the rules of evidence.

obligation
A responsibility that is morally and possibly legally binding. Although it is often used synonymously with duty, it is broader and includes both mandatory actions as well as the disposition or state of mind expected of the individual.

online counseling
Counseling or therapy by a licensed practitioner of a client that involves little or no face-to-face contact and where the process and content of the sessions is conducted through e-mail or other electronic, Internet-based formats.

opinion
Judge's statement of the decision reached in a case.

Oregon Death with Dignity Act of 1997
Passed by Oregon state legislature, it allows legal physician-assisted suicide under certain prescribed circumstances. Before agreeing to assist a patient with suicide, the physician must order a mental health evaluation

when he/she believes that the patient may be suffering from a psychiatric disorder or depression that causes impaired judgment.

organizational climate
The manifestation of an organization's culture and the way individuals characterize the organization's atmosphere with regard to procedures and practices.

organizational culture
Constellation of shared values, beliefs, customs, and actions that characterize an organization. Defines an organization's identity to those inside and outside it, and provides a guide to action for new situations. It is to an organization what personality is to an individual.

organizational ethics
The form of ethics that recognizes the impact of organizational factors and involves the intentional use of values to guide decision making in organizational systems. Unlike business ethics and professional ethics, which characteristically view a given ethical concern from an individual perspective, organizational ethics views the same ethical concerns from a systems perspective.

overdiagnosis
Diagnosis that is more severe than diagnostically justified, which is submitted to a third party payor as justification that the proposed treatment should be authorized and reimbursed.

pain and suffering
The kind of damages that an individual may receive for physical or mental anguish that results from a legal wrong done against him or her.

parens patriae
Legal doctrine that the government has the right to act as the parent to those unable to properly protect their own interests, such as children or the disabled.

parental alienation syndrome (PAS)
The condition wherein a child or children become alienated from the noncustodial parent as the result of manipulation by the custodial parent.

parental kidnaping
The situation in which a parent abducts a child, usually from the custodial parent, in violation of a court order. Practitioners who aid a parent in any way in this violation can be found guilty of being an accessory to the crime.

parental rights
Rights to legally claim a child and to make decisions for that child.

paternity suit
Lawsuit to establish fatherhood. Once established, it usually involves the duty to pay child support as well as the right to visitation.

peer consultation
A process of conferring with a colleague to ascertain how other reasonable, similarly trained practitioners would practice in the same set of circumstances.

peer review
Process by which a group of health care or mental health professionals voluntarily discuss, review, and evaluate their work for the purpose of professional growth and development.

perjury
Act of intentionally providing false testimony under oath.

person with a disability
Individual with a physical or mental impairment. According to the Americans with Disability Act, a disabled individual is someone (a) who has an impairment that substantially limits one or more of the major life activities, (b) who has a record of such impairment, or (c) who is regarded as having such an impairment.

personal ethics
The form of ethics that reflects an individual's internal sense of how he/she should live, what he/she should strive for, and serves as the basis for moral decisions or judgments guiding behavior. An individual's "moral compass" or conscience reflects these ethical beliefs and values.

petition
A written application for the purpose of redressing a wrong.

petitioner
Individuals who initiate a legal action to redress a wrong in hope that some relief is granted them. The individual who files the action is called a petitioner or plaintiff, whereas the respondent or defendant is the individual against whom the complaint is made.

philosophical ethics
Cf. *general ethics.*

physical abuse
An act that results in nonaccidental physical injury or trauma, for example, punching, beating, kicking, biting, burning, or otherwise harming another. Physical injury that is a result of unreasonable, severe corporal punishment or unjustifiable punishment.

physical safeguards
Safeguard required by HIPAA, which requires the protection of the integrity and security of the physical locations where protected health information is stored and accessed. For example, a facility is required to create and maintain retrievable exact copies of all electronic protected health information in case of an emergency.

plaintiff
Individual who files the initial papers in a lawsuit. Cf. *petitioner.*

Plato
Greek philosopher (428–348 B.C.) who is credited with the ethical viewpoint called Platonic ethics. Cf. *Platonic ethics.*

Platonic ethics
Ethical teaching attributed to Plato, which is characterized by harmony or ordered integration. Plato posited that the goal of life is to actualize one's true nature; he further contended that the highest good is a well-ordered life based on virtues. He designated four cardinal virtues: wisdom, courage, temperance, and justice, wherein justice links the individual with society.

plea
A formal allegation filed by a defendant in reply to the plaintiff's complaint or charges.

pleadings
Formal documents filed in a court action, which includes the plaintiff's complaint and the defendant's reply.

portability
The ability of practitioners licensed in one state to move to another state and have their licensing credentials accepted.

postmodern ethics
Ethical approach derived from postmodernism. Embraces ethical pluralism and the ethic of being. Emphasizes virtue and spirituality, the communal nature of ethics, and narrative thought as a way to understand the relationship between ethics and personal identity formation. Cf. *narrative ethics.*

potentially detrimental practitioner-client relationships
Practitioner-client relationships that involve serious potential or actual harmful or illegal interactions. A recent legal term similar to the ethical designation "dual relationship."

power
In a professional context, the ability for the practitioner to influence the behavior of the client.

power differential
In a counseling context, the innate differential of influence favoring the practitioner in practitioner-client relationships, which can be either beneficial or harmful to the client.

precedent
Authoritative court decisions addressing identical or similar questions of law. A previous court decision that must be relied on by a court faced with a case with identical facts. A published appeals court decision that controls or influences the decisions of other courts.

prediction of dangerousness
The process of determining the likelihood that a client will cause harm to self or others. Although accurate prediction of dangerousness currently remains elusive, the judiciary nevertheless expects mental health professionals to offer an opinion about the foreseeability of such behavior.

preliminary hearing
Hearing held to determine whether or not a probable cause for an arrest existed and an indictment in a criminal matter is warranted.

prima facie
Latin phrase that means "at face value"; a fact is presumed to be true if it is not rebutted or proven untrue.

principle ethics
Objectively applying a system of ethical rules and principles to determine what is the right decision when an ethical dilemma arises. It focuses on the objective, rational, and cognitive aspects of the decision-making process.

privacy
Right of individuals to have control over their personal information. More inclusive than confidentiality, which involves communication within the context of counseling.

privilege
Legal right to refuse to cooperate with a request for information, for example, a subpoena about confidential disclosures made by a client to certain professionals including attorneys, physicians, pastors, and, more recently, psychotherapists. The psychotherapist-client privilege was established by the U.S. Supreme Court in *Jaffe v. Redmond.*

privileged communication
Communication between certain professionals and clients that is protected by statute from forced disclosure to third parties. It includes the client's right to prevent a practitioner from revealing confidential information in a legal proceeding. There are some exceptions, such as when a law requires a psychotherapist to report illegal activity, such as child abuse.

profession
A collected body of individuals committed to acquiring specialized knowledge and skills in order to serve the needs of others, act in a competent and ethical manner, and has a self-governing organization that establishes standards of competency, ethics, and practice guidelines for the provision of services.

professional
A member of a profession who applies specialized knowledge and skills based on the profession's standards of excellence for meeting client's needs rather than merely advancing the professional's personal needs or interests.

professional and ethical decision making
Decision making in professional practice and ethical practice that involves a similar strategy and process. They are also interdependent in the sense that professional input and analysis (that is, research, best practices, theory, or clinical lore) are first considered and then ethical input (theory, values, principles, and codes) are considered in order to reinforce, refocus, or fine-tune the decision.

professional boundaries
Cf. *boundary.*

professional competence
The professional's capacity to provide a minimum quality of services rendered within the professional's and the profession's scope of practice. Such competence can be measured by what other reasonably prudent professionals would do under the same circumstances.

professional counseling
The practice of counseling by a professional based on the application of mental health, psychological, and human development principles through cognitive, affective, behavioral, and systemic intervention strategies that address issues of wellness, personal growth, and career development, as well as pathology.

professional ethics
The form of ethics that endeavors to help professionals decide what to do when they are confronted with a case or situation that raises an ethical question or moral problem; it considers the morality of one's professional choices and is informed by a code and standard of ethics specified by one's profession.

professional malpractice
A lawsuit brought against a professional alleging that the individual breached the duty of care owed to the client.

professional sanctions
Corrective measures delivered by a professional organization or certification or licensure board to one of its members, which can range from limitation of practice, a directive for supervision, or additional training. Failure to cooperate with the sanction can result in expulsion from membership or revocation of certification or licensure.

progress or psychotherapy notes
Notes written by a practitioner that document a client's progress, provide a record of events and interventions taken, and may serve as a means of communication among professionals working with the same client. Usually either problem-oriented, focused on progress made in addressing the problem, or goal-oriented, focused on progress made in reaching the treatment goal.

protected health information
Any information related to the client's condition or health status protected by law. Abbreviated as PHI.

psychological ethics
Approach to ethics that explores the psychological aspects of moral capacity and the process by which moral behavior develops. Cf. *moral development*.

psychological Miranda warning
A warning about the exceptions to confidentiality given by a practitioner to a client at the outset of treatment.

psychological testimony
Expert testimony of a mental health professional typically about a diagnostic condition, prognosis, intervention, treatment process, or progress.

psychosocial assessment
Report that contains a practitioner's assessment of a client in terms of psychosocial factors and functioning, including motivation for treatment, cognitive ability, social and family relationships, marital status, vocational/educational functioning, drug and alcohol use, and health factors.

psychotherapist-client privileged communication
Communications between a practitioner and a client wherein the practitioner cannot be forced to disclose such communications without the client's consent. Established as federal common law by the U.S. Supreme Court in *Jaffee v. Redmond.*

psychotherapy notes under HIPAA
Notes recorded by a practitioner that document or analyze a conversation with a client during a private, group, or family counseling session. It should include session start and stop times, modalities and frequency of services, clinical test results, and any summaries of diagnosis, functional status, the treatment plan, symptoms, prognosis, and progress.

punitive damages
Damages awarded to successful plaintiffs that are designed to punish or hurt defendants who have committed outrageous acts. Cf. *compensatory damages.*

qualified expert
Expert who, based on specialized training and experience, has been approved to testify in legal proceedings.

reasonable accommodation
Any modification or adjustment to a job or the work environment that will enable a qualified applicant or employee with a disability to participate in the application process or to perform essential job functions. It also includes adjustments to assure that a qualified individual with a disability has rights and privileges in employment equal to those of employees without disabilities.

reasonable care
Level of care that is expected of a professional in the execution of his or her duty by a sensible person or professional. Cf. *reasonable person standard*.

reasonable person standard
Level of care that is expected of a professional in the execution of his or her duty. Sensible persons and professionals can be expected to object when the standard of care is below this level.

reciprocity
The process whereby a licensed practitioner's credentials in one state are recognized by another state for licensure purposes without additionally imposed requirements.

recovered memory
A memory that was previously repressed and is now recovered and brought into consciousness years or decades after the event.

redress
Action to remedy, set right, make up for, or remove the cause of a complaint.

referral
Informing a client who needs treatment of the availability of professionals or treatment programs that can meet those needs.

regulation
An administrative rule that clarifies and explains laws passed by legislatures related to the mandate and mission of a government agency.

relational supervision
A process of supervision explicitly recognizing the situatedness of both supervisor and supervisee within larger domains of professional and social discourse and the influence of such discourse on the process and outcome of supervision.

relationship advocate
A mental health or legal professional who functions to mediate certain relationship issues such as the negotiation of a divorce settlement. The professional does not represent the interests of any one party but instead is an advocate for an equitable solution.

relativism
Assertion that all judgments, beliefs, opinions, and claims to truth are contextually conditioned. It assumes that the context of any discourse influences its outcome and that therefore there are no absolutes, universal norms, or ethical imperatives.

relief
Legal redress that a court grants a plaintiff in response to a request.

religion
The search for significance through the sacred, within the context of a shared belief system (doctrines), and communal ritual practice (liturgy or public worship).

remedy
Relief from a wrong or injury to which a plaintiff is entitled.

repressed memories
A theory about psychological materials that remain below the level of consciousness because of the pain such memories would cause at the conscious level. Often involves early experiences of sexual abuse. There is considerable controversy and little consensus about the validity of such memories.

respect for persons
The ethical value and principle that involves honoring the dignity, worth, individual differences, and rights of all individuals to privacy, confidentiality, and self-determination.

respondeat superior
Latin for "let the master answer," meaning that the master is responsible for the legal consequences of the acts of his servant. Cf. *respondeat superior doctrine*.

respondeat superior doctrine
Legal principle that holds that a superior is responsible for the negligent acts of subordinates and that assumes that the superior has control and directs the action of a subordinate. The doctrine by which clinical supervisors are held liable for the action of their supervisees.

responsibility
Condition in which an individual or organization is accountable or answerable for something. From an ethical perspective, it is viewed as including an obligation, some accountability for the obligation, and an ethical sense. More specifically, a practitioner's obligation or duty to clients and his/her profession to act in an appropriate and professional manner.

restraining order
Judicial order granted to benefit an abused or harassed individual, directing the abuser or harasser to stay away from the abused or harassed individual's residence or other places and to refrain from abusive, harassing, or stalking behavior.

restraint
Removing or restricting a person's voluntary movement or choice to act. Restraints can be "physical" or "chemical." A physical restraint involves a device (e.g., safety belts, safety bars, geriatric chairs, and bed rails) that restricts or limits voluntary movement and cannot be removed by the patient. Chemical restraint involves the use of medication or a chemical

to immobilize a person. Physical restraint is usually legally permissible when a person is clearly a danger to self or others.

revocation of licensure
Refers to the loss of the right to practice in the licensing jurisdiction, usually as a result of professional misconduct.

right to decline treatment or medication
Constitutionally based right of individuals to refuse medication and/or any treatment. The exercise of this right requires that the client or patient be competent to make such decisions.

rights ethics
The ethical theory that assumes that individuals are the bearers of rights that are granted them. An act is considered morally good and right when it respects rights, and wrong when it violates rights.

rights of children
Belief that because children are vulnerable they need to be protected from undue harm. Accordingly, they have the right to be provided with basic requirements for the growth and development of their physical and emotional health.

scope of employment
Refers to the role, responsibilities, and context of employment. With regard to clinical supervision, it means that a supervisor has the authority and responsibility to control his or her supervisee. It includes the supervisee's duty to perform a specific act; the time, place, and purpose of the supervisee's act; and the motivation of the supervisee in committing the act.

scope of practice
The extent and limits of professional activities by an individual who is licensed or certified and that is considered acceptable professional practice as defined by the profession or by statute. It also refers to a recognized area of proficiency, competence, or skills gained through appropriate education and experience.

security
Tools and safeguards through which the client's confidentiality is protected by the practitioner.

self-determination
Refers to the capacity and right of individuals to act as an agent on their own behalf and to direct their own future, including their own choices, actions, and cognitive/emotional behaviors.

self-referral
An individual who requests psychiatric, psychotherapeutic, or counseling services for himself/herself without a referral by another.

self-supervision
Active, ongoing conversations practitioners have with themselves about their clients, their own thinking about their clients, their clinical case conceptualizations, their assessments of their professional effectiveness, and their attention to the political and ethical effects of their own clinical formulations and interventions on their clients.

settlement
The resolution of a legal matter achieved by a compromise before litigation or final judgment, which eliminates the necessity of a trial.

sex offender
An individual who commits a sexual act prohibited by law.

sex with clients
A major ethical and legal violation involving sexual activity between a practitioner and a client that effectively violates the boundaries of the therapeutic relationship and seriously compromises clinical objectivity and efficacy.

sexual abuse
A form of abuse involving any type of sexual conduct directed at a minor by an adult or an older minor.

sexual exploitation
The taking of nonconsensual, unjust sexual advantage of another for one's benefit or the benefit of another party. Such an act may or may not be accompanied by the use of coercion, intimidation, or through advantage gained by the use of alcohol or other drugs.

sexual harassment
Persistent and unwanted sexual advances or sexually related activities usually initiated by a senior and more dominant individual that is directed at a junior and weaker individual in a workplace or academic setting.

sexual misconduct
Any physical act of a sexual nature perpetrated against an individual without consent or when an individual is unable to freely give consent. It encompasses a range of behaviors, from inappropriate touching to rape. It also includes sexual exploitation. Cf. *sexual exploitation.*

90

sexual misconduct in a professional relationship
The crossing of an appropriate sexual boundary with a client in violation of the practitioner's code of professional ethics and/or legal statutes to which the practitioner is subject.

situation ethics
Ethical approach in which love is posited as the principle governing moral action and that all other ethical principles and laws are secondary considerations. It is situational in its assumption that the form the principle of love takes in a given situation cannot be determined by abstract reasoning apart from or before the situation itself.

slander
False oral statement, made in the presence of a third person, that injures the character or reputation of another.

slippery slope argument
Argument that a certain course of action will eventually lead to the erosion of all moral restraint. In counseling or therapeutic settings, it is the belief that small "innocent" boundary crossings will eventually result in gross, exploitive ones, such as sexual contact with clients.

SOAP notes
A four-section progress or psychotherapy note in which each letter of the acronym represents a section of the note: "S" (subjective) contains the information given to the practitioner by the client during the session, "O" (objective) contains the factual information observed directly by the practitioner, "A" (assessment) contains the practitioner's impression of the client, and "P" (plan) contains the plan for treatment and the practitioner's prognosis for the client.

social ethics
Ethical reflection emphasizing social strictures and processes and how specific social contexts influence and shape moral behavior. Contrasted with personal ethics.

sole custody
To have the right to make decisions and to have physical custody of a child; therefore being the custodial parent with the right to receive support on behalf of the child. Being a sole custodian does not mean having sole responsibility. Sole custodians usually receive child support.

special damages
Damages that are unique to a case that are added as a result of the nature of a particular case.

spiritual interventions
Interventions that address a client's spiritual dimension or issues and that are either alternative or complementary counseling interventions or both.

spiritual sensitivity
The capacity to be aware of and to recognize the importance and/or influence of religious or spiritual beliefs, values, and other factors on another's life.

spirituality
That unsatisfiable, deepest desire within everyone, and the ways individuals deal with that desire: how they think, feel, act, and interact in their quest to satisfy this unsatisfiable desire; the transcendent aspect of life that gives a sense of meaning and purpose to our lives.

spousal abuse
Domestic violence directed by one spouse against the other.

standard of care
A description of the conduct expected of an average member of the profession practicing within his/her specialty, and which is a measure against which a defendant's professional conduct is compared.

statute
A law or act passed by the legislative branch of government.

statute of limitations
A statute specifying the time period within which litigation must be initiated for a particular cause of action.

statutory law
Law that is prescribed by legislative enactments. Because statutes always appear in print form, they are referred to as "black letter law."

stay away order
A protective order that specifies the distance that a designated individual, for example, abuser, batterer, or stalker, must remain from the home and workplace of the individual obtaining the order. Also known as a restraining order.

stipulation
An agreement made by opposing attorneys concerning any matter involved in the legal proceedings. Typically in writing, it is binding if agreed on by both parties.

strict liability
A legal theory that anyone creating a condition of extreme hazard should be liable for the harm caused by that hazard, and that the normal requirement that the injured plaintiff prove negligence or bad intentions should be waived. Liability that is imposed just because the harmful act was done.

subpoena
A legal document requiring the recipient to appear at a legal proceeding and/or to provide specific information or documents. Disregarding it may result in being held "in contempt of court" and subject to a punishment.

subpoena duces tecum
A legal document that requires the recipient to appear at a deposition or in court at a specified time, place, and date with a specific set of records that are requested directly in the subpoena.

suicide
The act of killing oneself.

suit
A proceeding in a court of law initiated by a plaintiff.

summary of judgment
A court's decision to settle a dispute or dispose of a case promptly without conducting full legal proceedings.

summons
Court order that directs an appropriate official to notify the defendant that a civil lawsuit has been filed and the court and date on which the defendant must appear.

supervision
An intervention provided by a member of a profession to a less experienced member of that same profession. It is evaluative, extends over time, and has the purposes of enhancing the professional functioning of the more junior person, monitoring the quality of the services offered to clients, and serving as a gatekeeper for entrance into the profession.

supervision guidelines
Specific guidelines for supervision issued by licensing boards and professional organizations, which set forth the requirements for supervisor qualifications and responsibilities as well as supervisee qualifications and responsibilities. Such guidelines can be admissible in a court action to show the minimum standard of care required and whether a supervisee or supervisor has breached his/her duty to the client.

supervisor impairment
Incapacity to perform the function of the supervisory role because of a debilitating medical, substance-related, or psychological condition that results in diminished functioning.

supervisor incompetence
The incapacity to perform the function of the supervisory role due to a lack of training, experience, unwillingness, or inflexibility.

support order
Legal requirement that one individual pays a specified amount of money, goods, or services to another, as in child support.

supreme court
The highest level of appeals court that reviews and reconciles conflicting decisions of lower appeals courts within its jurisdiction. In the United States, each state has a supreme court, whereas the U.S. Supreme Court, the highest level of federal court, has jurisdiction over all the state supreme courts, and its decisions become the law of the land.

surrogate decision maker
Individual who has been designated to make decisions on behalf of an individual determined incapable of making his/her own decisions.

surrogate mother
Woman engaged to bear the child of a man not married to her in order to produce a baby for that man and his infertile wife.

suspension of licensure
A temporary loss of the right to practice a profession within a jurisdiction.

synderesis
Term used to designate the first principles of moral action. Sometimes used synonymously with conscience but differs: it is the grasp of moral principles and knowledge, whereas conscience is a broader concept that applies these general principles and knowledge to specific situations.

Tarasoff doctrine
The legal duty, based on *Tarasoff v. Regents of the University of California* ruling for mental health practitioners, to warn and protect identifiable victims of the danger posed to them by a client of the mental health practitioner if such a danger is reasonably foreseeable and imminent.

Tarasoff duty
The practitioner's duty to warn and protect an intended victim of threats made by a client. It is an exception to the practitioner-client privilege that originated in California courts and has been adopted by most jurisdictions. However, it does not have a mandatory reporting requirement.

technical safeguards
Specific safeguards required by HIPAA that require the creation and implementation of policies and procedures to protect electronic health information from unauthorized access, alteration, or destruction. For example, a facility may employ software that can protect against viruses or corruption to protect client information. Cf. *Health Insurance Portability and Accountability Act.*

termination hearing
A legal hearing to consider terminating specific personal or property rights. For example, such a hearing on parental rights decides whether

the best interests of a child will be served by severing the ties between the biological parents and the child.

testifying expert
An expert who is identified as a potential expert witness for trial.

therapeutic contract
A client-practitioner contract usually outlining intended treatment, payment terms, and exceptions to confidentiality. This becomes effective when the agreement is signed or understanding reached usually during the first session. In crises or emergency situations, it begins when professional contact is made.

third party
An individual or organization such as a relative, a referral source, or a payor who is involved with a clinical case but who is neither the practitioner nor the client.

third party rule
Legal rule that states that when two individuals converse in the presence of an unrelated third person, there is no expectation of privacy and no confidentiality. This rule affects legal confidentiality in family and group therapy.

threats to others
In the counseling context, refers to threats against the physical safety of third parties made by clients to practitioners.

tort
A civil wrong, other than a breach of contract, done by one individual to another. A tort requires (a) a legal duty owed by one individual to another, (b) a breach of that duty, and (c) harm done as a direct or indirect result of such action. In the counseling context, actions for negligence and malpractice are examples of tort actions.

trial
The examination of a civil or criminal case by a judge or judges. It may or may not involve a jury.

trial court
A court that first hears a case. It applies existing laws to the facts presented by the litigants. It is not allowed to modify those laws and its decisions are usually not published and are not precedents.

umbrella rule
Legal concept permitting all professionals employed in a mental health agency to have some access to confidential client information while imposing confidentiality obligations on all such access. It is the basis on which secretaries and administrators of such agencies can work with files irrespective of whether they are trained practitioners.

undue hardship
Legal doctrine that in making a reasonable accommodation for disabled employees, employers are not expected or required to endure significant hardships in conducting business, either financially or architecturally.

undue influence
Influence over another that destroys that individual's choice or voluntary action. It is considered unprofessional, unethical, and possibly illegal, depending on the circumstances.

unethical
Action that violates or does not conform to approved standards of social or professional behavior. Can be intentional or unintentional. Often undetected because only the individual committing the violation may be aware of it.

universal moral judgments
Ethical or moral assertions believed to be applicable in all situations and circumstances. It can be linked to the principle of universality or the universalizability axiom, which is a restatement of the categorical imperative. Another way of describing this axiom states: "What is right or wrong for a particular person is right or wrong for any similar person in all similar circumstances." It contrasts with relativism.

upcoding
Diagnosing a client with a more serious or severe diagnosis that may be diagnostically unjustified.

U.S. Supreme Court
Cf. *Supreme Court.*

utilitarianism
Cf. *consequential ethics.*

vacate
The action of canceling or rescinding a court decision.

value judgment
Assertion that ascribes goodness or worth to a person, a state of being, a character trait, or an object. In ethical discourse, it can be contrasted with judgments of obligation, which are declarations of what one ought to be or do.

value system
A particular hierarchy or rank-ordering of preference for the values expressed by a particular individual, organization, or community. A group of social norms that guide human behavior in a given group, organization, or community.

values
Personal convictions, beliefs, and opinions that shape attitudes and motivate behavior. The quality that makes something desirable, useful, and worthwhile.

valuing
Process of negotiating values with a client. Imputing worth to an act or condition.

venue
Geographic area or site in which an action or case is tried.

verdict
Formal declaration of a jury's finding of fact that is signed by the jury foreman and presented to the court.

vicarious liability
Supervisor's liability that results from the negligent acts of supervisees if the acts are performed in the course and scope of the supervisory relationship. It may involve neglectful or intentional acts and is based on the theory that the supervisor violated a direct duty to know what his/her supervisees were doing and to control their conduct.

virtue
Habitual, well-established readiness or disposition directing an individual to some goodness of act; the quality of being morally good or righteous.

virtue ethics
The ethical theory in which ethics is primarily about internal dispositions and character rather than external behavior or actions. Basic to this theory is the assumption that virtues make one a morally good person.

visitation
The right to have visits with one's children at specified times, usually granted to the noncustodial parent.

voluntariness in informed consent
Agreement by clients of their own free will and without undue influence to receive the treatment that has been duly explained to them.

wage attachment action
A legal request ordering the employer of a defendant who is behind in child support payments to deduct the payment from wages, which the court can then direct to the plaintiff.

waiver
Voluntary relinquishment of an individual's rights. For example, a client can waive privilege, which permits his/her practitioner to testify to information that ordinarily would be protected, confidential communication.

Web counseling
The practice of professional counseling and information delivery over the Internet. Also called Internet counseling. Cf. *cybercounseling* and *online counseling*.

whistle-blowing
Reporting of unethical behavior or illegal activity.

witness
Individual who gives testimony under oath in court.

work orientation
Refers to a view and attitude toward work as determined by intrinsic values and aspirations and the experience of working that is reflected in thoughts, feelings, and behavior about work.

work product
Confidential notes and documents used by attorneys in preparing a case that is protected by privilege and is sometimes applied to other professions. A practitioner's journal in which he/she reflects on a case may qualify as a work product.

workers' compensation
Payment provided to disabled workers.

wrongful commitment
A cause of action brought against a practitioner for committing a patient to a psychiatric unit or institution in violation of some rule or legal test. It can constitute false imprisonment or unlawful detention.

Part II
Ethical Issues and Considerations

Mental health professionals regularly face professional situations involving ethical issues, ethical dilemmas, or other ethical considerations. This handbook is intended to be a "ready reference" for the most common ethical issues and considerations professional face in everyday practice. Part II has been designed to provide you with key points about such issues and considerations. It describes each issue or consideration directly and concisely. Because the language of ethics tends to be rather technical, we have endeavored to make Part II as user-friendly as possible. To save you the time and effort of looking up specific terms in the Dictionary section of this book, we have included definitions of key terms relevant to each topic right in the discussion of each ethical issue. Clinical applications of each topic are described and guidelines are presented. The following ethical issues and considerations are discussed in this section.

- Boundaries, Boundary Crossing, and Violations
- Competence (Practitioner)
- Community Values and Ethical Decision Making
- Complementary and Alternative Counseling
- Confidentiality
- Cultural Factors in Ethical Decision Making
- Ethical Decision-Making Strategy
- Ethical Perspectives and Professional Practice
- Ethical Theories Impacting Professional Practice
- Ethics Audit of an Organization or Clinical Practice

- Informed Consent
- Internet Counseling
- Organizational Ethics
- Religion, Spirituality, and Ethics
- Technology and Ethics
- Using Case Material in Presentations and Publications

BOUNDARIES, BOUNDARY CROSSINGS, AND VIOLATIONS

The issues of boundaries and boundary violations are increasingly important today. In fact, boundary issues—which are integrally related the issues of dual relationships and conflicts of interest—have become a critical concern in the ethical and professional practice of counseling and therapy for both trainees and experienced practitioners. The reason is primarily because of the inherently vulnerable position of clients in counseling or therapy. By exposing their emotional, cognitive, and interpersonal needs and difficulties during treatment, clients are in a position of reduced power and greater vulnerability in relationship to the practitioner. Accordingly, practitioners have the ethical obligation to be conscious of this power differential and client vulnerability and to act in accordance with ethical principles that promote the client's well-being and best interests. As already noted, boundary considerations are associated with two related ethical considerations—conflicts of interest and dual or multiple relationships—and, thus, all three are considered here.

Terms and Related Considerations

Boundary
A boundary can be defined as the frame and limits surrounding a therapeutic relationship that specifies a set of roles and rules for relating for both client and therapist. Because of a power differential between client and therapist and because clients are in a vulnerable position and boundaries serve to protect the client's welfare, the concept of boundary is central to understanding conflicts of interest and involves two polar positions: the categorical boundaries view and the dimensional boundary view in which boundary crossings and boundary violations are a major point of contention. The distinction between boundary violation and boundary crossing is essential for practitio-

ners in their evaluation of ethical considerations involving their relationship with a client or possible intervention goals and strategies.

Categorical Boundaries View

The view that boundaries are part of human interaction with the purpose of delineating role functions and of facilitating the therapeutic process. In this view, boundaries in professional relationships are considered immutable, not open to debate, and should not be crossed for any reason. Furthermore, such boundary crossings are viewed as a slippery slope that eventually result in serious boundary violations.

Dimensional Boundaries View

The view that although professional relationships involve power differentials, relationships are not inherently abusive or exploitive. Even though boundaries are useful and necessary in professional relationships, they can be discussed openly by mental health professional and client, and boundary crossings, when appropriate, can facilitate the therapeutic relationship and treatment outcomes.

Boundary Crossing

A boundary crossing is a benign and typically beneficial departure from traditional expectations about the settings and constraint of clinical practice. Boundary crossings involve any deviation of clinical behavior from the standards of practice associated with traditional or conservative treatment approaches that emphasize emotional distance or reducing clinical risk and liability. Examples include accompanying a claustrophobic client in riding up and down in a small elevator during exposure therapy or greeting a Hispanic client with an embrace—a culturally sensitive practice. Although frowned on by advocates of psychoanalysis and risk management, such crossings are commonly accepted in many humanistic, behavioral, and systemic forms of psychotherapy. There is evidence that boundary crossings may promote both the therapeutic alliance and positive client outcomes.

Boundary Violation

Boundary violations are exploitive or harmful practices in psychotherapy that occur when therapists cross standards of professional behavior for their own sexual, emotional, or financial gain. Examples include becoming sexually involved with a client, entering into a business partnership with a client, or confiding personal information to a client to satisfy the practitioner's own emotional needs.

105

Conflict of Interest

A conflict of interest arises when a practitioner has competing interests that would get in the way of faithfully exercising his or her professional judgment and skill in working with clients. An example would be a client who came for treatment seeking brief therapy for a focal concern to a practitioner was more comfortable practicing longer-term therapy. Rather than referring that client to someone who would confidently provide such brief treatment, the client begins seeing that client anyway because his case load was open and he was paying his son's college expenses. The practitioner's judgment could be affected by a competing concern to fill his caseload and pay his bills. When a practitioner's needs and interests prevail, that is, come before the client's needs, interests and overall welfare, abuse of power and boundary violations are warning signs or indicators of a potential conflict.

Dual or Multiple Relationship

Dual relationships involve both a professional role and relationship, that is, therapeutic or supervisory, alongside a personal, social, business, or other or non-professional role and relationship. The term "multiple relationship" is also used to described two or more types of relationships occurring between a practitioner and a client. For example, a practitioner who provides therapy to an individual and rents an apartment to that client is involved in a dual relationship: client-practitioner relationship and a landlord-tenant relationship. Although dual relationships are not inherently wrong or conflicting, they do involve the risk of abuse or misuse of power as well as loss of objectivity.

Guidelines for Evaluating Boundaries and Relationship Issues

Because of the importance of boundary and relationships issues in clinical practice, practitioners would do well to carefully consider the nature and scope of their relationships with clients. Here are some guidelines to consider when dealing with boundary and relationship issues:

- Review what the code of ethics of your professional association and/ or state or federal laws say about the particular situation.
- Determine what ethical principle(s) guiding clinical behavior would be helpful in deciding what the best course of action to take might be in the particular situation.
- Consider the circumstances from the perspective of your theoretical approach or clinical model.

- Assess the particular issue or circumstance from the perspective of power differential between yourself and the client.
- Determine what other influences might be operative in your ethical decision-making at this time such as financial concerns; cultural differences; personal, family, or relational problems; or experiencing isolation or loneliness that could influence your judgment.
- Consider whether it would be helpful to seek supervision or consultation from trusted colleagues about this particular situation.

COMPETENCE (PRACTITIONER)

Clients expect that the practitioners with whom they consult will be competent. But what exactly does competence mean in the mental health professions? Competency is about capability and performance and can be defined as sufficiency in reference to an external standard. Sufficiency in counseling and psychotherapy refers to the capability to provide counseling and clinical services responsibly and proficiently within one's scope of practice, while external standards include legal statutes, regulations, and professional codes of conduct. Competence is much more than completing graduate training and achieving professional certification or licensure. Rather, competence is an ongoing developmental process in which an initial level of competence is achieved and maintained and then updated and enhanced as new developments arise and the profession and the professional grows and changes. Failure of competence may involve incompetence or impairment, which can be reflected in negligence.

Terms and Related Considerations

Competence
Competence refers to a practitioner's capability to provide a minimum quality of service within the professional's and his or her profession's scope of practice. For legal purposes, competence is measured by what other reasonably prudent practitioners would do under the same circumstances.

Scope of Practice
Scope of practice is a legal designation specified in licensure laws. It can be defined as the extent and limits of activities considered acceptable professional practice by an individual who is licensed or certified in a

profession. More specifically, it refers to a recognized area of proficiency in professional practice involving specific competence, proficiency, or skills acquired through appropriate education and experience.

Incompetence

Incompetence can be defined as the incapacity to perform the function of the counseling role because of insufficient training or experience, unwillingness, or inflexibility.

Impairment

Impairment can be defined as the incapacity to perform the function of the counseling role due to a debilitating medical, substance-related, or psychological condition that results in diminished functioning from a previous higher level of functioning. Distress and burnout can lead to impairment.

Negligence

Negligence involves a failure on the professional's part to exercise foresight in performing a service. Negligence also can involve a lack of proper care of an omission or commission of an act that a reasonably prudent professional would or would not do under the given circumstances. Negligence is often described as dereliction, that is, providing a reasonable standard of care, of a duty that directly causes damages.

Malpractice

Malpractice is a violation of a professional duty or duties expected of a reasonably prudent professional and involves performing below the professional standard of care. Malpractice is a form of negligence. To prevail in a malpractice suit, four basic elements—the four D's—must be established. They are: dereliction of duty directly causing damages.

Ethics Codes and Standards

The ACA, APA, AAMFT, and NASW codes of ethics and standards address competence. These codes emphasize the importance of developing and maintaining professional competence. Overall, they highlight the importance of practicing within the boundaries of knowledge and skill (i.e., scope of practice). These codes also acknowledge that it is possible to extend one's scope of practice but only after obtaining additional training and supervised experience. Finally, they specify continuing education or ongoing efforts to maintain competence.

Achieving and Maintaining Competence

Attaining Competence

Competence develops over time as a result of several educational experiences: didactic instruction, discussion, reading, supervised experience, and appropriate professional experience. For most practitioners, the process of becoming competent to engage in professional practice begins with graduate training. Accordingly, graduate faculty and supervisors bear the initial responsibility for producing competent professionals.

Maintaining Competence

Once trainees have completed their formal training and are licensed or certified to practice, the responsibility for ensuring competence shifts away from educators and supervisors to the professionals themselves. As independent professionals, they are expected to assume the burden for monitoring their own effectiveness and the scope of their practice.

Continuing Education

Because of the proliferation of new theories and knowledge, counseling approaches, and assessment and intervention strategies, it appears that it would be impossible for a counselor or therapist to maintain more than a modicum of professional competence over the course of their professional career without additional education and training. There are several venues for increasing competence; these include formal education such as ongoing supervision, seminars, workshops, or other training that issues continuing education credits (CEUs). Most credentialing bodies have established continuing education requirements to maintain certification or licensure.

Guidelines Regarding Competence

- Limit the scope of your practice only within the boundaries of their competence, based on their education, training, supervised experience, state and national professional credentials, and appropriate professional experience.
- Expand the scope of one's practice, that is, practice of new approaches or new specialty areas, only after appropriate education, training,

and supervised experience. When developing skills in new specialty areas, take steps to ensure the competence of your work and to protect others from possible harm.

- Accept employment only for positions for which you are qualified by education, training, supervised experience, state and national professional credentials, and appropriate professional experience.
- Monitor your effectiveness, continuously, as a professional and take steps to improve when necessary.
- Seek continuing education to maintain a reasonable level of awareness of current scientific and professional information in their fields of activity. Take steps to maintain competence in the skills you use, be open to new procedures, and keep current with the diverse and/or special populations with whom you work.
- Refrain from offering or providing professional services when your physical, mental, or emotional problems are likely to harm a client or others. Stay alert to the signs of impairment, seek assistance for your problems, and if necessary, limit, suspend, or terminate your professional responsibilities.
- Foster competence by adopting professional and personal self-care strategies.

COMMUNITY VALUES AND ETHICAL DECISION MAKING

Values are understood as what is considered good and desirable to an individual or a group, and ethos refers to the fundamental character or the underlying sentiment that informs the ideals, beliefs, and norms of a community or society. As used in this book, the term "community values" refers to the ideals, beliefs, norms, and ethos that arouse an emotional response for or against them in a given community. The phrase "emotional response for or against" is key in this definition. In short, community values reflect the sentiments of what the majority of a community consider important, good, and desirable and influence their decisions and actions when their values are at stake. Considering the influence of community values—among other contextual considerations—is an important step in the ethical decision-making process. Failure to consider how community values about mental health-related issues and policies could or did impact ethical dilemmas or considerations could have unfortunate short- and/or long-term consequences.

Terms and Related Considerations

Community Values

Refers to the ideals, beliefs, norms, and ethos that arouse an emotional response for or against them in a given community.

Organizational Ethics

The form of ethics that recognizes the impact of organizational factors and involves the intentional use of values to guide decision making in organizational systems. Unlike business ethics and professional ethics, which characteristically view a given ethical concern from an individual perspective, organizational ethics views the same ethical concerns from a systems perspective.

Ethical Sensitivity

The capacity to recognize situations and circumstances—including organizational, cultural, and community factors and dynamics—which have implications for the welfare or well being of another. Ethical awareness is a prerequisite for ethical sensitivity.

Impact of Community Values

Although some community values may be well articulated and openly discussed and others are not necessarily articulated, communities will go to great lengths to safeguard what they hold as important and good. The perception that such community values are being compromised or threatened tends to provoke a defensive response in the community. Depending on the extent of that response, members and/or community leaders may take decisive action to "protect" the community from the actual or perceived threat.

Examples of community values and efforts to safeguard them abound. Voters in some towns and geographical areas may consistently vote down school referendums, whereas in other communities such referendums will be overwhelmingly approved because such expenditures are considered consistent with that community's valuing of children and educational advancement. Some communities are quite accepting and accommodating of homeless individuals, whereas other communities express their impatience and disdain for such individuals by expecting that loitering statutes will be enforced. Similarly, depending on its values, communities may or may not be receptive to the need for access to and provision of

111

adequate treatment for the disabled and mentally ill and thus will predictably approve or disapprove initiatives for funding of services.

Recognizing and understanding community dynamics and values is essential in making specific informed ethical decisions, as well as in evaluating the "fit" between an individual professional and the community in which he/she is training or working or is considering training or working. Such an investigation of community dynamics and values also can provide a plan for advocating and modifying community values.

Guidelines for Identifying Community Values

- Identify sources or markers of community values. Chief among these is the local newspaper(s). Analyze its "op-ed" page or section, which includes letters to the editor and editorial opinions on local matters. It usually also contains one or more regular columns by national or local columnists.
- Expressed opinions and editorial in such newspapers may closely reflect community values or it may not at all. Determine this by asking a dozen different individuals in that community how they view their local newspaper.
- Assess the larger community's opinion about a particular agency or clinic or the local school system, or about particular leaders or newsmakers in that organization. Compare the community's comments about that organization or a leader's reputation and the "actions" the community takes about that organization or individual in terms of financially and/or emotionally supporting it.

COMPLEMENTARY AND ALTERNATIVE COUNSELING

In the past decade, there has been increasing interest in alternative medicine and complementary medicine (CAM). Surveys indicate that more than two-thirds of adults in the United States have utilized CAM, with the 1-year prevalence rate of 42%. Furthermore, interest in complementary and alternative counseling (CAC) is increasing. Just as there are ethical and legal issues associated with CAM, it should not be surprising that appear to be some unique ethical and legal considerations associated with CAC, including spiritual counseling interventions. Common CAC interventions include meditation, guided imagery, praying with clients, yoga, herbal remedies, and other New Age interventions. This section reviews definitions of relevant terms and related considerations, then briefly describes common ethical and legal issues, as well as practice guidelines related to CAC.

Terms and Related Considerations

Alternative Medicine
The utilization of medical or healing methods and interventions that are outside the usual and customary pattern of medical practice in place of conventional or mainstream medical interventions. This differs from complementary medicine.

Complementary Medicine
The utilization of alternative medical or healing methods alongside or in conjunction with conventional medical interventions.

Complementary and Alternative Medicine
A recent term that blurs the distinction between alternative medicine and complementary medicine. It is often designated as CAM.

Alternative Counseling
Approach to counseling that involves interventions and models of treatment that are outside the usual and conventional purview of professional counseling practice.

Complementary and Alternative Counseling
An approach to counseling that involves alternative counseling interventions that are utilized alongside or in conjunction with usual and traditional counseling interventions. It is often designated as CAC.

Spiritual Interventions
Interventions that address a client's spiritual dimension or issues and that are either alternative or complementary counseling interventions or both.

Scope of Practice
The extent and limits of professional activities by an individual who is licensed or certified and that is considered acceptable professional practice as defined by the profession or by statute. It also refers to a recognized

area of proficiency, competence, or skills gained through appropriate education and experience.

Malpractice

Violation of a professional duty expected of a reasonably prudent practitioner and involves performing below the professional standard of care. It is a form of negligence, which requires four specific elements to be met. Thus, to prove a case of negligence, the plaintiff must show that at the time of the alleged negligent incident, a legal duty between the practitioner and the client existed, the practitioner breached that duty, and that the client suffered harm or injury that was directly and proximately caused by the practitioner's breach of duty.

Informed Consent to Treatment

The client's right to decide whether to participate in treatment after the practitioner fully describes the services to be rendered in a manner that is understandable by the client.

Theoretical and Practical Considerations with CAC

When it comes to integrating CAC into conventional practice, at least five dilemmas confront the practitioner. First, there is an insufficient research base for making evidence-based decisions about treating conditions with CAC. Second, when such research-based information does exist, the practitioner may be unaware of the safety and effectiveness of such interventions because graduate training has, historically, not included CAC topics. Third, many CAC interventions have philosophical underpinnings that challenge orthodox counseling perspectives, and thus hinder attempts at scientific validation with conventional methodologies. Similarly, practitioners typically have not been adequately educated about the scope of practice, licensing requirements, and credentialing of CAC practice, which raises concerns about client safety and legal liability when recommending alternative and complementary approaches or therapists. Finally, and most relevant to this discussion, practitioners may be uncertain about how to translate well-established principles of professional ethics into this new domain of practice.

Ethical, Legal, and Regulatory Issues Involving CAC

Even though CAM seems quite different from conventional medicine, when it comes to ethical and legal matters, there appear to be few differences between CAM and conventional medicine. With regard to CAC practice and conventional counseling practice, the same generalization can be made. That being said, there are however, there are some unique considerations with regard to inadequate informed consent, licensure and scope of practice, and malpractice liability for negligent practice and referral.

Informed Consent

Informed consent is perhaps the most important ethical and legal consideration regarding CAC. It requires practitioners to be responsible to inform clients about treatment options, including risks and benefits. Does that mean that practitioners are obligated to discuss complementary interventions? The answer is "yes," given that CAC is a viable treatment alternative for a particular client. The principle of autonomy requires that clients have sufficient understanding to make autonomous decisions, and thus practitioners are expected to provide information about all relevant treatment options. Withholding information, or not being knowledgeable enough to provide complete information, seriously undermines not only trust but also the client's ability to offer informed consent as well as client autonomy. Accordingly, informed consent obligates practitioners to provide clients all the information that is relevant to a decision to consent to or forgo a specific intervention or course of treatment. However, this can be problematic given the rapid growth in the breadth and depth of psychological knowledge, particularly about CAC interventions. Because practitioners are increasingly unlikely to know about all potentially relevant treatment options, they may unintentionally fail to provide complete information. Accordingly, practitioners would do well to keep abreast of current trends in conventional and CAC interventions through their professional reading and CEU courses.

The ethical principle of nonmaleficence that is, not doing or allowing harm to a client, also must be considered when discussing CAC options and recommending nutritional supplements such as herbal remedies or regressive interventions such as primal therapy as untoward effects have been reported for these and other CAC interventions. Assessing and communicating risks and benefits can also help manage liability concerns. Although practitioners are not obligated to provide CAC services, they must be familiar with local practitioners who can provide such treatment options and to whom they can make referrals.

Licensure and Scope of Practice

Given that a complementary and alternative intervention is appropriate and the client consents to such an intervention or course of treatment, the question arises as to whether the practitioner has the authority to provide that service. Because certification or licensure is a matter of state law, there is great diversity among the states as to who can be licensed, and the scope of practice allowed for the provision of CAC services. Most jurisdictions require practitioners to have a minimal level of competence in specialized modalities such as CAC through training and/or supervised experience, to provide professional services outside the original scope of practice for which they have been certified or licensed. Needless to say, as most practitioners have not been trained and supervised in CAC interventions, it is incumbent on them to seek such training and experience, or be prepared to refer clients to practitioners who have such competence.

Malpractice Liability for CAC Treatment

Just as with conventional modalities and interventions, practitioners face malpractice liability for negligent practice of CAC. Even practitioners who have competence in CAC can be found negligent in providing such services. Guidelines for reducing malpractice liability can be found in the "Malpractice" section in Part III of this book. Surprisingly, there is considerable amount of case law concerning negligent practice of CAC, particularly spiritually related interventions. The interested reader can consult Ronald Bullis's *Sacred Calling, Secular Accountability: Law and Ethics in Complementary and Spiritual Counseling* (Brunner/Mazel, 2001) for an extensive account.

Another issue confronting practitioners is the extent to which they have liability connected with referring clients to CAC providers. Generally speaking, a straightforward referral to a specialist should not leave the referring practitioner liable for subsequent negligence by that specialist. However, there are some exceptions. The first involves referral wherein that the referring practitioner knew or "should have known" that the CAC provider might be "incompetent." A second exception involves "joint treatment" of the client, in which the practitioner and CAC provider share information by telephone or e-mail as part of the treatment plan. The possibility of such shared liability suggests exercising great care in selecting CAC providers to whom one will refer, as well as the risks of the CAC treatment and/or its interaction with conventional care.

Guidelines for Consideration of CAC Interventions

- Become familiar with the growing scientific evidence concerning the safety and effectiveness of relevant complementary, as well as mainstream, therapies.
- Assess client attitudes and beliefs toward CAC and expectations for treatment.
- Evaluate your own attitudes toward CAC and ethical analysis.
- Know relevant professional guidelines and the ethical principles of autonomy, nonmaleficence, beneficence, and justice.
- Apply common sense to balance the risks and benefits of any therapy before recommending a course of action, and continue to monitor patients appropriately.
- Discuss with clients any information that is relevant to treatment decisions, whether treatment options involve conventional or CAC therapies.
- Consider how to negotiate decisions and particular views, with emphasis on effective communication with the client. This is particularly important when discussing risks and benefits. Achieving mutual collaboration not only increases the therapeutic alliance but decreases the likelihood of client dissatisfaction and malpractice.

CONFIDENTIALITY

The Hippocratic Oath states: "Whatsoever things I see or hear concerning the life of men, in my attendance on the sick or even apart therefrom, which ought not be noised abroad, I will keep silence thereon, counting such things are sacred secrets." Confidentiality is the cornerstone of the counseling and psychotherapeutic process, and arises from an ethics of care that values the privacy and autonomy of clients. Confidentiality provides the framework within which clients can disclose and explore aspects of themselves and their relationships that are problematic, personally painful, and that might cause embarrassment or harm if known outside the counseling relationship. Essentially, confidentiality insures that the counseling process is safe for the client. If clients were not provided the professional and legal protection of confidentiality within the counseling relationship, it would be hard to imagine why individuals would seek out counseling or psychotherapy. For all practical purposes, the success of the counseling and therapy process depends on the development of a relationship of trust and caring, and confidentiality is essential in fostering such a relationship.

Confidentiality and Related Considerations

Confidentiality

The obligation of practitioners or therapists to respect the privacy of clients by not revealing to others the information communicated to them by clients during counseling sessions. In couples and family therapy, it is granted primarily to the whole (e.g., family) rather than to the individual, unless otherwise stated.

Privileged Communication

Privileged communication refers generally to the embodiment in statute of the right to privacy of communications between psychotherapist and client, and freedom from forced disclosure, except as specified by law. In granting privilege to psychotherapeutic communications, society—through the judicial system—acknowledges the importance of privacy in psychotherapy for it to be effective and the chilling effect on mental health professionals that forced or unwanted disclosures would have. Affording privilege to psychotherapeutic communications also implicitly recognizes psychotherapy as a social good that improves the health and well-being of people. Individual states define and extend psychotherapeutic privilege differently and also the exceptions to privilege.

Informed Consent

The client's right to base their decision about participating in counseling or clinical services—which includes assessment and interventions—after such services have been adequately described and explained in a manner that is understandable to the client. Information about the proposed services should include the purpose, risks and benefits, and possible alternative treatments, including the option of no treatment, as well an adequate description of exceptions to confidentiality and, where appropriate, what kind of reporting is required for court-ordered or mandatorily referred clients.

Health Insurance Portability and Accountability Act (HIPAA)

The provisions of HIPAA require that organizations that provide medical or psychotherapy services must be responsible and accountable for the policies and procedures they use to protect clients' private health information. Individual mental health care providers must safeguard the privacy of counseling and psychotherapy assessments, treatment plans, and progress notes. However, the umbrella agency or organization also must account for the standards it uses to safeguard these records. HIPAA was designed to provide a uniform and consistent set of procedures across the United States for protecting health information. This standardization was deemed necessary in order to inspire patient and client confidence in the handling of their private health information, especially in this era of electronic database storage and instantaneous transmission of data.

Exceptions to Confidentiality

Mandatory Reporting

Physical and sexual abuse of minors, disabled adults, and the elderly are serious situations in which therapists in most jurisdictions are required by law to provide mandatory reports of such abuse. Most states or jurisdictions have a hotline or reporting agency where reports of abuse are directed. Generally, the reporting laws require that professionals have a mandatory obligation to report the abuse of a member of a vulnerable population. The reporting requirement usually describes the need to report in situations where the professional either knows of suspects that abuse has occurred. In most jurisdictions, professionals who report abuse in "good faith" are protected from civil lawsuits for breach of confidentiality. Abuse reporting does not usually require that the professional have proof of abuse, but rather that the professional has good reason, within the parameters of professional competence, to suspect that abuse is happening.

Suicide and Confidentiality

The ethical codes of the ACA, AAMFT, NASW, and APA all obligate their members to breach confidentiality and to act on behalf of saving their client's life in the event of clear and imminent danger of suicide. This obligation is related to specific ethical values, particularly beneficence and autonomy. In order to protect a client's life (beneficence), his or her freedom (autonomy) may need to be restricted temporarily. In the case of involuntary hospitalization of a suicidal client, the client's autonomy is severely restricted in order to promote the client's survival and therefore well-being, and also to promote the opportunity for recovery from the depression and impaired reasoning usually associated with suicide.

Threats to Others and Confidentiality

In the *Tarasoff v. The Regents of the University of California* (1974, 1976) case, the courts held that the right to privacy of psychotherapy patients is limited if they make threats to harm others. The case is used illustratively in counseling training programs to point out that confidentiality does not extend to threats to harm other made by clients in therapy, and that further, the psychotherapist has a duty to protect a third party if a threat against that third party is made by notifying the third party of the threat. Subsequent court rulings have clarified the *Tarasoff* decision suggesting that violating client confidentiality is legitimate only when there is a specific intended victim and when the stated intent is to harm that specific victim. In most, but not all states, such as Florida, Tarasoff-type statutes requiring mandatory reporting are in place.

Minors and Confidentiality

The most salient dilemma in considering the rights of children to confidentiality is the potential tension between a child's right to privacy and a parent's right to know. In general, children are not afforded a legal right to confidentiality but the issue is debated in the professional literature. Cultural beliefs and values about the nature of the parent-child relationship and who should handle sensitive information are primary considerations for the ethical counselor.

Guidelines for Insuring Confidentiality

- Know the exact confidentiality requirements for mandatory report in your state or jurisdiction.
- Endeavor to develop and maintain a high level of trust and communication with your clients. This includes providing ongoing information to your client about the treatment process.
- Ensure that your "Consent for Treatment" form contains a clear and detailed description of exceptions to confidentiality and the duty to report suspected child abuse, elder abuse, or abuse of disabled persons to the Department of Children and Families or its equivalent in your jurisdiction. Note that informed consent begins rather than ends with the signed consent form.
- Remember that ongoing informed consent enhances and strengthens the client-therapist relationship and confidentiality. After the

client has signed the "Consent for Treatment" form and before the formal counseling session begins, ask the client if he or she has any questions about any part of the "Consent for Treatment" form.

- Recall that practitioners are required to obtain written permission in order to release confidential counseling records to third parties, except in the case of emergencies.

CULTURAL FACTORS IN ETHICAL DECISION MAKING

Diversity and the multicultural dimension are increasingly important today. The term "multicultural" can be understood in a broad or narrow way. Narrowly, multicultural represents race or ethnicity. Broadly, it includes race or ethnicity, as well as gender, age, economic status, nationality, disability, sexual orientation, and religion and spirituality. It also includes organizational and community values and dynamics. Although practitioners may be limited by their experiences in these various groups, they are nevertheless expected to recognize and respect diversity, in their effort to promote the welfare, respect, and dignity of their clients. Today, professionals have become increasingly aware that when practitioners and clients are from different cultural groups, differences may exist between them related to values, perception of situations, and even styles of communication. Furthermore, they are learning that even the counseling process may be uncomfortable and unacceptable to clients from some cultural backgrounds.

Terms and Related Considerations

Multicultural
Understood broadly, it refers factors such as ethnicity, nationality, economic status, gender, age, disability, sexual orientation, and religion and spirituality that impact the counseling process.

Cultural Competence
The capability for awareness of cultural dynamics and values, for tolerance of ambiguity, and for collaboration and utilization of culturally sensitive interventions.

Cultural Encapsulation
A tendency for practitioners to treat clients and others relative to their own cultural perspective, without regard to their clients' cultural differences.

Cultural Sensitivity
The capability to recognize and appreciate differences in cultural values, mores, and practices in individuals and groups of other ethnicities and cultures.

Ethical Sensitivity
The capacity to recognize situations and circumstances—including organizational, cultural, and community factors and dynamics—which have implications for the welfare or well being of another. Ethical awareness is a prerequisite for ethical sensitivity.

Community Values
Refers to the ideals, beliefs, norms, and ethos that arouse an emotional response for or against them in a given community.

Organizational Ethics
The form of ethics that recognizes the impact of organizational factors and involves the intentional use of values to guide decision making in organizational systems.

Culturally Sensitive Practice

Effective practitioners practice in a culturally sensitive manner. A key characteristic of culturally sensitive practice is cultural competence. A major contribution to the counseling and mental health professions has been the development of multicultural competencies such as:

1. Demonstrate an awareness of one's own culture and openness toward other cultural value.
2. Know and understand the client's culture.
3. Collaborate with key individuals from the culture to support the client, as well as seek support for oneself and consultation on cultural issue.
4. Utilize interventions that have been adapted to client need or interventions designed for cross-cultural counseling.
5. Develop and demonstrate a tolerance for ambiguity.

The Primacy of Cultural Awareness

Of these five competencies, the first—the capacity to manifest or demonstrate awareness of one's own culture as well as openness toward other cultural value—may be the most difficult for many practitioners. Why? The problem is "cultural encapsulation," a kind of cultural tunnel vision. Over 40 years ago, Wrenn (1962) described the culturally encapsulated practitioners as those who define reality according to their own set of cultural assumptions, are insensitive to the cultural values of others, and are, for all practical purposes, trapped in their own way of thinking that resists adaptation and rejects alternatives. Today, many trainees enter graduate school in mental health specialties with such cultural tunnel vision. Because of limited cultural experiences, they may unwittingly impose their cultural values on other trainees and clients. The solution to the problem of cultural encapsulation is cultural sensitivity. For this reason, it is imperative that counseling and psychotherapy training programs foster and expect cultural sensitivity from its faculty, staff, and trainees.

A practitioner's own cultural identity, acculturation, religious, and spiritual values, and gender role socialization—which can be thought of as the practitioner's cultural worldview—can significantly affect his or her perception of a client's situation and circumstances. When it comes to ethical issues, the practitioner's cultural worldview can frame a given situation as an ethical dilemma or not. Not surprisingly, the practitioner's level of awareness of one's own cultural worldview is an operative factor in ethical dilemmas.

Guidelines for Considering Cultural Factors in Ethical Decision Making

- Collect relevant cultural information such as immigration, family values, religious and spiritual values, and community relationships, as it impacts the problem.
- Determine the key participants involve based on the cultural values of the clients.
- Determine whether the identification of the courses of action involve in the dilemma reflect the counselor's cultural worldview, the client's, or both.
- Evaluate the extent of cultural sensitivity of your professional ethical code; and estimate the potential conflict between laws and ethical codes from a cultural perspective.

- Ensure that the courses of action selected reflects the culture world-views of the participants involved.
- Use relational methods to reach agreement on potential courses of action.
- Identify culturally relevant resources and strategies for the implementation of the decision and plan.
- Anticipate cultural, personal, and organizational barriers to successful implementation of the plan.

ETHICAL DECISION-MAKING STRATEGY

Good ethical practice can and should reflect effective professional practice, and effective professional practice can and should reflect good ethical practice. One implication of this way of thinking about ethical and professional practice is that ethical practice and professional practice are interrelated, and can be thought of as two sides of the same coin. Another implication is that the decision-making process in both is similar, with some aspects of the process being essentially the same. Practitioners employ similar decision-making processes whether it primarily involves a professional practice issue or an ethical practice issue. Whether the practitioner's decision making is intuitive and immediate, or is intentional and takes more time, a decision is reached after some kind of consideration of contextual, professional, and ethical factors. However, because many practitioners have been socialized to think of ethical decision making as unique and separate from clinical or professional decision making, the similarities may not be intuitively obvious. Nevertheless, there is considerable value in combining professional input and analysis, that is, research, best practices, theory, or clinical lore, with ethical input, that is, theory, values, principles, and codes, are considered in order to reinforce, refocus, or fine-tune the professional input and analysis. The ethical decisional strategy described here combines these both these dimensions.

Terms and Related Considerations

Ethical Decision-Making Strategy

A method for making decisions about ethical issues or dilemmas. Strategies tend to be linear or nonlinear. Linear strategies analyze data in terms

124

of linear process involving specific steps: defining the issue or problem, specifying alternative courses of action, seeking input from relevant ethical codes and legal statutes, seeking consultation from peer and/or experts, deciding on a course of action, implementing and evaluating the decision. Nonlinear strategies utilize similar steps but emphasize the integration of contextual, professional, and ethical considerations rather than just ethical and legal considerations.

Ethical Dilemma

Situations involving an ethical consideration that perplex a professional either because there are competing or conflicting ethical standards that apply, or there is a conflict between and ethical and moral standards.

Professional Considerations

Input from several sources: the research literature, including evidence-based studies, best practices, and the like, as well as counseling theories, scholarly debate and clinical lore, that is, clinical observations or methods that not empirically support but are revered and passed down from generation to generation.

Ethical Considerations

Begins with the basic ethical principle that acting in the best interest of client is the main criteria for determining the goodness and effectiveness of counseling, includes applicable codes of ethics and standards of practice (that is ACA, APA, ASCA, etc.).

Contextual Considerations

Any cultural, organizational, community, interpersonal, or personal dynamics that are operating.

Collaborative Decision Making

Includes therapists and practitioners and their client and client's family and/or social network, where appropriate, in cooperative conversations to identify problems and develop treatment plans and strategies to address them. Collaborative decision making also includes all key stakeholders in making decisions about the nature of treatment, options to treatment, whether treatment is effective or not, and when to terminate treatment.

125

Approaches to Ethical Decision Making

Whether a professional or ethical decision is instantaneous or takes a few minutes or more, all practitioners engage in some decision making process. Several models of ethical reasoning exist in the literature. The simplest is an informal approach that begins with information about a client's situation and is initially evaluated by the practitioner's immediate impression, that is, intuitive moral sense of the right thing to do. This intuitive sense can then be evaluated at a critical level, that is, evaluating the client situation in terms of general ethical principles, ethical theory, and professional codes, then weighing alternatives, considering possible outcomes, and evaluating the impact of their decisions. More formal decision-making approaches have been described. The majority of these involve a linear, rational decision-making framework based on a problem-solving protocol: identify the problem, specify alternatives, evaluate each alternative, and decide on the best alternative. Most practitioners have been taught such a linear, problem-solving approach. There also are a few nonlinear approaches, the best of which broaden the context of ethical thinking beyond immediate circumstances, simplistic calculations, or a single ethical standard or legal statute. The approach described here is based on a broad, integrative, contextual analysis.

Guidelines for Effective Ethical Decision Making

An integrative, nonlinear decisional strategy is described here that emphasizes professional, contextual, and ethical factors. It is an eight-step process in which the initial step (0) of the decision-making strategy is a general and ongoing process—one of increasing one's ethical sensitivity and anticipating professional-ethical considerations—rather than specific to a given ethical problem or dilemma.

0. Enhance ethical sensitivity and anticipate professional-ethical considerations
1. Identify the problem
   - Is there an ethical dilemma here? If so, how do you define it?
   - What facts of the case lead you to define it this way?
2. Identify the participants affected by the decision
   - Which individuals are directly involved? Indirectly involved?
   - How are you being affected by it? Your client(s)? Others?

126

3. Identify potential courses of action and benefits and risk for the participants
   - What potential options or courses of action can you identify?
   - What are the risks and benefits of each course of action for each participant?
4. Evaluate benefits and risks with regard to key contextual, professional, and ethical considerations
   - What's your ethical sense or intuition about the case?
   - How might your personal values be operative here?
   - How is your level of professional developmental and ethical perspective operative here?
   - How might your blind spots, unfinished business, or countertransference be operative?
   - What is the level of trust and mutuality in the client and other participants?
   - What, if any, ethnic, gender, or cultural factors are operative?
   - What are the spiritual/religious beliefs of the client and what is their influence?
   - What are the stated versus actual core organizational or institutional values?
   - What is the community's attitude toward and impact on the dilemma?
   - What is the relevant standard of care in the community?
   - If applicable, what do research, best practices, and so on have to say?
   - What is the prevailing scholarly opinion about this issue?
   - What does clinical lore, that is, the counseling tradition, say about it?
   - What theory(ies), ethical value(s), and ethical principle(s) are applicable in this case?
   - Which professional codes are applicable? Standards?
   - Are any legal statutes applicable? If so, which one(s)?
5. Consult with peer and experts
   - What views do your supervisor(s), colleagues, lawyers, and so on suggest in resolving the dilemma?
   - If different from ethical standards and principles, how is it different?
6. Decide on the most feasible option and document decision-making process and rationale

- Are the original options still viable or is revision necessary?
- What is the best option? What's your rationale for it?
- Should you inform your supervisor or an administrator of the decision?

7. Implement, evaluate, and document the enacted decision
   - How should you implement the decision?
   - What is the result of the various ethical tests: publicity, universality, moral traces, and justice?
   - How will you document the decision, process, and rationale?

ETHICAL PERSPECTIVES AND PROFESSIONAL PRACTICE

The professional behavior of mental health practitioners is informed by various perspectives individuals have of professional and ethical situations. Three perspectives characterize the current practice of counseling and psychotherapy, and three such perspectives or views have been described. Irrespective of years of experience or professional discipline, practitioners can be characterized by two polar views or perspectives on the relationship of professional ethics and professional practice. One view is that ethics and professional practice are integrally linked, whereas the other view is that they are distinctly separate. For those who view the two as integrally linked, sound professional practice is considered highly ethical practice because ethical values "inform" professional practice. Accordingly, ethical values are consistent with best practices, research, clinical lore, and professional experience, but when there is potential conflict, ethical values "trump" clinical lore, or clinical experience. This contrasts with the view that ethics is separate from professional practice and that ethics is merely an add-on or isolated consideration, rather than an integral consideration in professional practice decisions.

Terms and Related Considerations

Perspective I
An ethical viewpoint in which individuals tend to perceive their professional activities and the focus of ethical thinking in terms of ethical codes, ethical standards, and legal statutes. Complying with enforceable rules and standards, managing risk, and avoiding censure are high priorities in this perspective. Specifically, this means avoiding prohibited

and "slippery slope" behaviors, such as boundary crossings, and instead engaging in risk management activities that reduce the likelihood of malpractice and/or professional censure. Ethical sensitivity means awareness of professional misconduct, ethical problems, and ethical dilemmas. For the most part, one's personal and professional ethics are separated.

Perspective II

Ethical viewpoint that represents a midway position between Perspectives I and III. Professional practitioners operating from this perspective recognize that increasing competence is valuable either in terms of advancing their career or because the notion of being a lifelong learner has some appeal. Individuals here tend to view their professional work as either a career or a calling. To the extent to which their goal is to advance their career, they will become involved in informal and formal continuing education efforts. They also become involved in continuing education activities because they recognize that their work involves making a difference in others' lives. Their involvement in continuing education efforts is more intense and active compared to those embodying Perspective I but not with the intensity or commitment of those in Perspective III. Self-care and wellness are more likely to be a reactive response to distress or burnout rather than a proactive initiative. Individuals embodying this perspective are more likely to function in adequate or proficient stages of competence.

For many professionals, this perspective is a transition phase to Perspective III. It represents an effort to comply with ethical standards and rules, while at the same time expressing some willingness to consider self-reflection, contextual considerations, and self-care. The extent to which individuals holding this perspective experience cognitive and emotional dissonance is a function of how much allegiance they have to Perspective I: the more allegiance, the less dissonance, and vice versa. Although these individuals may express some interest in integrating their personal and professional values, there is little commitment to such an effort.

Perspective III

Ethical viewpoint in which individuals perceive competence as an ongoing, developmental process. Generally speaking, individuals here view their professional work as a calling. Accordingly, they are very invested in their work and it provides them considerable job satisfaction as well as life satisfaction. Admittedly, they take the responsibility of monitoring their level of competence seriously, and welcome opportunities to increase their expertise. Supervision, case consultation, and continuing education programs are important avenues for enhancing knowledge and skills. Although some of these individuals are voracious readers and consumers of the professional and research literature in their field, most others manage to find a way to stay current with new developments. These practitioners often are sought out by others for supervision and consultation, roles to which they take seriously and are likely to have attained a high level of proficiency. Self-care is valued and considered essential in this perspective because it is believed that as professionals take care of themselves they are better able to care for others. Self-care and wellness are more likely to be a proactive rather than a reactive response. Not surprisingly, these individuals tend to be viewed by their peers as master therapists.

The Transition from Perspective I to Perspective III

As professional ethics became part of the training of practitioners in the late 1970s and early 1980s, it would be fair to say the Perspective I was the dominant mode in both teaching and in professional practice. Although Perspective I remains common today, particularly among trainees and beginning practitioners, Perspective II probably reflects the sentiments of an increasing number of practitioners today. Perspective III seems to reflect other trends in the field involving consolidation and integration, that is, integrative therapies, incorporating the multicultural and spiritual dimension in treatment, and so on. Recent research suggests that master therapists live and model a growth-based, positive ethics that is characteristic of Perspective III. As such, they provide a useful and necessary example of professional practice to other aspiring practitioners.

A basic premise is that the natural progression from beginning to advanced to master therapist and counselor involves movement from Perspective I or II to Perspective III.

Although these three perspectives appear to be discrete, it must be pointed out that ethical standards and legal statutes are not "confined" to Perspective I. All practitioners, irrespective of the particular perspective they espouse, are expected to provide services reflecting a basic standard of care and mandatory ethical codes and standards. It can be usefully to identify the perspective that informs your clinical practice and that of others.

Guidelines for Utilizing the Three Perspectives

- Markers of Perspective I are observable in an individual's professional behavior and actions: views ethical and professional practice as separate; attends primarily to mandatory ethics, that is, standards and statutes; guided by legal sensitivity and risk management consideration; separates personal and professional life.
- Markers of Perspective III are observable in an individual's professional behavior and actions: views ethical and professional practice as integrated; attends primarily to ethical values and aspiration ethics while mindful of standards and statutes; guided by ethical sensitivity while mindfulness of the need to minimize risk; integrates personal and professional life.
- Markers of Perspective II reveal aspects of both Perspectives I and III.

ETHICAL THEORIES IMPACTING PROFESSIONAL PRACTICE

The actions of practitioners are guided by their ethical perspectives and these ethical perspectives reflect one or more ethical theories. Whether or not they are aware of and understand their preferred ethical theory, this theory influences practitioners' ethical decision making. An ethical theory is a framework for understanding and dealing with ethical considerations. It is the way in which an individual's values are acted out in the world. An ethical theory is the way one chooses to live out and interpret one's values. An ethical theory considers one's underlying values and provides a means of determining which values take priority in any given situation. Such a theory is the means by which individuals can interpret and apply their values in the world. In other words, it is the way a practitioner puts into practice the choices made about what is valuable in his or her profession. Such theories have at least two purposes. The first is to provide an orientation toward ethical situations. Such a theory involves a set of assumptions about how ethical situations ought to be addressed, and which component of an ethical situation takes priority. The second purpose is to resolve conflicts among standards and values. When standards come into conflict or when competing values cannot both be acted on, an ethical theory provides a hierarchy of values to evaluate this conflict and provide a rationale and defense for one's decision. In sum, it enables one to resolve ethical dilemmas and defend the solutions reached. It is a framework that the practitioner brings to his or her ethical experience, to the living of his or her professional and personal lives against the backdrop of a commitment to values.

For many practitioners, this theory is implicit, meaning that whereas it guides one's actions, it is not consciously recognized or understood. Accordingly, it is advantageous for practitioners to recognize, understand, and appreciate the theories that guide their thoughts and actions in making decisions in counseling practice. Six common theories are briefly described here.

Terms and Related Considerations

Consequentialist Ethics

This theory aims at realizing the best possible consequences. An act is considered good and right only if it tends to produce more good consequences than bad consequences for everyone involved. Operating from a consequentialist perspective is relatively straightforward. First, consider the available options. Second, list what particular persons are affected, either positively or negatively, by each option. Third, assess the degree of good or harm that will likely result to each of the persons under each of the options. This can be accomplished by quantifying the worth or even by assigning a numerical figure to the good or harm that comes to each person. For example, using a scaling technique, that is, where 1 is considerable harm and 10 is considerable good, rate each option for each person. Fourth, evaluate the ratings for all individuals and choose the right action that brings about the most good than harm.

Rights Ethics

Theory that assumes that individuals are the bearers of rights that are granted to them. An act is considered morally good and right when it respects rights and wrong when it violates rights. Operating from a rights theory typically involves the following considerations. First, the rights theorist would consider whose rights are at issue. Then he/she would determine how to preserve and uphold these rights. Although it may not be immediately obvious which option is best in terms of upholding rights, the rights theorist would assess which rights are overriding or whose rights take precedence. Finally, the rights theorist reflects on the situation and the individuals involved and arrives at the alternative that does the best job of honoring rights. He/she would have to decide whose integrity or privacy ought to count more and which rights are more fundamental. But this decision is not particularly easy or straightforward given a number of questions that arise: Is the right to integrity more basic than the right to equal treatment? Which rights must be satisfied first? What rights do individuals really have, since individuals can claim a right to something that they do not actually have? Who decides what rights individuals have? Where do rights come from? These are difficult questions facing rights theorists.

Duty Ethics

Theory that considers the intention of the person choosing, the means, and the nature of the act itself. An act is considered morally good and right if it is done for the sake of duty, has a good motive, its means are acceptable, and/or the nature of the act itself is good. Operating from a duty theory typically involves the following considerations. First, the duty theory counts as relevant many aspects of a moral situation, such as the motive, the means, the nature of the act, and even, for some duty theorists, the consequences. Second, it is valuable to look at all of the aspects of a moral situation before deciding which aspect of the situation is overriding. Third, duty theory also respects the dignity of individuals and the obligations owed to them. It does not endorse permitting the good of all to always supersede the good of a particular individual. For duty theory, a duty or promise to a single person can be more morally compelling than good consequences to a whole community. An example of duty ethics is psychiatrists and investigative reporters who refuse to divulge information about clients and sources, even when faced with arguments claiming that the good of the community depends on having that information.

Virtue Ethics

This theory defines virtues as that which makes one a morally good person. Ethics and morality are understood primarily in terms of internal dispositions and character rather than external behavior or actions. Operating from a virtue ethics theory typically involves the following considerations. First, the virtue theorist identifies which virtues are at stake in a situation. Next, he/she considers how each option would or would not realize the virtues. Then he/she chooses the course of action that expresses either more virtues or the more important virtue. Unfortunately, the virtue theorist cannot automatically discern whether loyalty to one's boss or justice to one's colleagues is the better choice. To provide

133

a fuller ethical perspective, virtue ethics needs guidance from other ethical theories. For example, it would seem that a virtue whose expression affects more individuals would be preferable to the expression of a virtue that affects only a single individual. Expressing benevolence to many individuals would seem preferable to expressing benevolence to one. Furthermore, it would seem that a choice that expresses many virtues may be preferable to a decision that realizes only a few virtues. In this way, consequentialism provides guidance to virtue theory. Consequentialism informs the virtue theorist that realizing more virtues is better than realizing fewer virtues, and that those virtues that have an effect on more people are more important than those that have an effect on fewer people. Conceivably, a virtue theorist could rank the virtues or decide that in certain relationships the virtues must be expressed first toward some individuals and only later toward others. For instance, virtue theorists can claim that individuals should pay back a loan before giving gifts to their friends, or to act in ways that benefit one's parents before acting to benefit oneself or one's friends.

Care Ethics
Theory that is rooted in persons and relationships, wherein ethical decisions are made by focusing on relationships rather than on actions, duties, or consequences. An act is considered morally good and right if it expresses care or is done to maintain a caring relationship. Originally, care theory was articulated by women and premised on the observation that females tend to be more focused on relationships, whereas males tend to be more focused on rules. Operating from a care ethics theory typically involves the following considerations.

First, and foremost, it means finding ways to foster the expression of care and to sustain relationships. Second, it means avoiding embarrassment, neglect, and harm and instead seeking to express care toward the greatest number of people, including individuals that most need or deserve care. Although this theory seems straightforwardly altruistic, it raises some interesting questions: Is it better to express more care to a few individuals or to express some care toward more individuals? Are certain individuals more deserving of care than others? Another concern with care theory is that in its early forms it was modeled on the maternal figure, which many regard as the personification of the caring, nurturing person.

Narrative Ethics

Theory that insists that narrative or story and its context are important in ethical decision making. An act is considered morally good and right if it reflects the ongoing story of an individual's life, culture, and tradition within which he or she lives it. Operating from narrative ethics theory typically involves the following considerations. First, narrative theorist attempts to understand the context, the histories, and beliefs of the individuals who find themselves in a particular situation. Important considerations include: the individual's childhood history, education and training, family and professional roles, career aspiration, successes and failure, beliefs and core values, previous decisions, the laws, traditions, and cultural practices of the organization in which the individual is affiliated. Such information about the context of an ethical situation helps understand the life stories of the characters in it. Second, mindful of this information available about individuals' lives and cultural traditions, the narrative theorist endeavors to make decisions made will best fit the individual's needs and circumstances.

Knowing and Utilizing Your Dominant Ethical Theory

Earlier in this book, it was suggested that practitioners have a preference for a particular ethical theory, and that even if they are unaware of their preferred theory, it can have a dominant influence on their ethical considerations and decision making. It should be noted that a practitioner's theory is distinguished not by one's actions but, rather, by how one decides how he/she will act in a given situation. For instance, someone operating from a consequentialist theory can be distinguished from someone with a care ethic by understanding why they decided to do what they did. Furthermore, some practitioners have a preference for two different theories. Interestingly, some theories are particularly compatible with others. For example, a practitioner with a preference for duty ethics may find it helpful to consider consequences along with duties. Similarly, a practitioner with a narrative ethics perspective may find they need a virtue theory or rights theory in order to have a standard or goal for their clients to strive toward in their life stories.

It is useful to take to the time to recognize and understand one's dominant ethical theory. Remember that even though one theory may be dominant, a practitioner can choose another theory or decide to use different theories in different situations when circumstances favor one theory over another. The guidelines below suggest some strategies for identifying your dominant ethical theory as well as for utilizing your knowledge of ethical theory in working with others.

Guidelines for Identifying and Utilizing Theories in Ethical Decision Making

- To identify which theory is dominant in your ethical deliberations and decision making, carefully review the six different ethical theories. Then, recall important ethical considerations or dilemmas that you faced and consider which theory was operative in your deliberations and decision making. Also, consider which of the theories that you most identify with or which seems to make the most sense to you. There may be two such theories that dominate your ethical thinking process.
- Ethical theories provide insight into ethical thinking of others as well. Try to identify the dominant ethical theory of those with whom you work. If you know that your supervisor or administrator values a consequentialist theory, you can expect that consequential reasons will be especially compelling to him.
- Because specific ethical values are associated with each ethical theory, knowing someone's ethical theory is indicative of the values he/she deems important. For instance, beneficence and nonmaleficence are highly valued by consequentialists, whereas beneficence and compassion are more highly valued by those with care ethic orientation.
- There are times when combining the insights from two or more theories can be helpful or even necessary in ethical decision making. Certain value conflicts may be best dealt with by a duty orientation, whereas other ethical situations call for a virtue ethics perspective.

ETHICS AUDIT OF AN ORGANIZATION OR CLINICAL PRACTICE

An ethics audit is an audit or investigation in which the implementation of ethical policies as well as ethical incidents in an organizational setting are reviewed and evaluated. In a counseling setting, ethics audits can be helpful in evaluating the adequacy of current ethics-related practices in the organization, modify practices as needed, as well as in monitoring the implementation of these changes. Ethics audits first emerged in the 1980s in corporate settings as a response to various corporate scandals. In for-profit corporations, ethics audits are routinely completed by accounting firms. In short, it is an investigation of how an organization's ethical policies are implemented as well as a review and evaluation ethical incidents occurring in an organization during a given time frame. Recently, ethics audits have been introduced in health care organizations and human services agencies either because of accreditation requirements or because of a culture of accountability that managed care and total quality assurance movement require. In the field of mental health, Reamer (2000) has advocated that ethics audits should be required in social work training and practice.

Such an audit can be performed by an outside consultant or by an inside consultant, typically, an external consultant who conducts interviews and surveys and reviews the organization's documents and documentation of ethics policy implementation and incidences. A standardized assessment device is utilized for identifying and reviewing pertinent ethical issues. Such a standard measure permits "benchmarking" or comparing results across organizations that have similar missions and structures. More informally, it can simply involve a brief review of the organization's core values, ethics policies, and ethical practices as they relate to professional ethical codes and standards by the use of short paper and pencil survey or inventory.

Terms and Related Considerations

Ethics Audit

An audit or investigation in which the implementation of ethical policies as well as ethical incidents in an organizational setting are reviewed and evaluated.

Organizational Ethics

The form of ethics that recognizes the impact of systemic or organizational factors and involves the intentional use of values to guide decision making in organizational systems. Unlike business ethics and professional ethics, which characteristically view a given ethical concern from an individual perspective or the perspective of a profession, organizational ethics views the same ethical concerns from a systems perspective.

Compliance Audit

Type of audit that determines the degree to which the organization's ethics meets the minimum standards set forth in legal statutes, regulations and policy, and the given profession's codes. Human services agencies tend to use this type which assesses the extent to which mental health providers and agencies have procedures in place to identify ethics-related risks and prevent ethics complaints and ethics-related litigation. Common factors assessed include: ethical risks, client rights, confidentiality and privacy, informed consent, service delivery, boundary issues and conflicts of interest, documentation, defamation of character, client records, supervision, staff development and training, consultation, client referral, fraud, termination of services and client abandonment, practitioner impairment, and the ethical decision-making process and method utilized by staff.

Cultural Audit

Type of audit that assesses how employees or staff feel about the standards and behavior of the organization. Cultural audits assess perceived priorities and ethical effectiveness of individuals, groups, units, or the organization as a whole.

Systems Audit

Type of audit that assesses compliance and culture as part of a bigger whole, namely, the degree to which the ethical principles, guidelines, and processes of the organization are integrated within the organizational system. Systems audits view the organization as a system and examine the ethics issues within that system, and between that system and critical elements of the environment within which it operates. They examine the relationships within and between several components: environment, resources, core values, mission and strategic goals, and individual values as they relate to legal, regulatory, policy, and professional ethics.

Ethics Audit in Clinical Practice

Why should practitioners consider performing an ethical audit of their professional practice? The main reason is that the organizational dynamics of a clinic school or agency can significantly impact the ethical and professional behaviors as well the job satisfaction of practitioners. Recently, the question of why it is that otherwise good and well-regarded practitioners engage in unethical and even illegal behavior in their professional setting has been an increasing but puzzling reality to many. Organizational ethics has come to prominence in the past decade largely as a result of corporate scandals, and it is now just entering the vocabulary of the health and mental health professions. Not surprisingly, ethical audits are a tool of organizations ethics.

An early finding in the study of organizational dynamics and ethics is that organizations that have well-articulated ethical values, principles, and professional standards and that act on these values, principles, and standards tend to foster both positive counseling outcomes in clients and personal and professional development and job satisfaction among staff better than organizations that do not. Staff commitment is likely to be higher, turnover is likely to be lower, and quality counseling outcomes are likely to result. This is particularly the case when a counseling intern's or school counselor's core ethical values and the school's actual ethical values are consistent. By contrast, the less positive and healthy the ethical culture or climate of a clinical organization, the more likely that practitioners will experience work-related stress. Accordingly, an evaluation of organizational ethics, particularly a compliance ethical audit, can be a useful tool to assess the ethical climate of the particular clinic, school, or agency in which you work or might consider working.

Guidelines for an Ethics Audit

- Evaluate your practice in terms of whether the organization: (1) has a formal ethics policy stating ethical values, principles, and professional standards; (2) has a commitment to its core values, ethical policies, and professional standards; and (3) has a high degree of correspondence between its stated values and its actual values as assessed by its staff.
- Evaluate your practice in terms of staff: (1) understanding and agreeing with the organization's core values and ethical expectations; (2) being listened to by administration when they identify ethical concerns about any aspect of their work; (3) and clients being treated with respect, fairness, and equality.
- Evaluate your practice in terms of whether: (1) ethical behavior is recognized and rewarded while immoral and unethical behavior is sanctioned; (2) confidentiality and client privacy is effectively safeguarded; (3) professional competency is highly valued and rewarded; (4) appropriate boundaries are maintained and harmful conflicts of interest are avoided; (5) informed consent is provided initially and

on an ongoing basis to clients; and (6) there are formal processes in place for staff to report suspected unethical behavior and/or to ask questions to clarify understanding of the ethics policies and standards without fear.

INFORMED CONSENT

Informed consent is a relational process between counselor and client that includes much more than just a signed and witnessed document. Informed consent typically unfolds in a four-part process. The first part of the process involves the client reading an information sheet or booklet outlining the elements of the informed consent document. The second part, assuming a well-trained practitioner, involves asking the client if he or she has any questions about any of the ideas covered in the informed consent document and includes the counselor summarizing the meaning of informed consent. The third part involves the client attesting to his or her understanding of informed consent by signing the informed consent document which is usually witnessed by the counselor or, on occasion, by an intake worker. The fourth part of the process is the ongoing manner in which practitioners inform their clients of developments or options as treatment progresses. This four-part process is key to effective professional conduct because it highlights the ongoing collaborative relationship between professional and client, particularly collaborative decision making.

Terms and Related Considerations

Informed Consent
The client's right to base their decision about participating in counseling or therapy services—which includes assessment and interventions— after such services have been adequately described and explained in a manner that is understandable to the client. Information about the proposed services should include the purpose, risks, and benefits, and possible alternative treatments, including the option of no treatment, as well an adequate description of exceptions to confidentiality and, where appropriate, what kind of reporting is required for court-ordered or mandatorily referred clients.

Confidentiality

The obligation of practitioners or therapists to respect the privacy of clients by not revealing to others the information communicated to them by clients during counseling sessions. In couples and family therapy, it is granted primarily to the whole (e.g., family) rather than to the individual, unless otherwise stated.

Privileged Communication

Privileged communication refers generally to the embodiment in statute of the right to privacy of communications between psychotherapist and client, and freedom from forced disclosure, except as specified by law. In granting privilege to psychotherapeutic communications, society—through the judicial system—acknowledges the importance of privacy in psychotherapy for it to be effective and the chilling effect on mental health professionals that forced or unwanted disclosures would have. Affording privilege to psychotherapeutic communications also implicitly recognizes psychotherapy as a social good that improves the health and well-being of people. Individual states define and extend psychotherapeutic privilege differently and also the exceptions to privilege.

Key Elements of an Ethically Sound Informed Consent Document

- Nature of the treatment to be provided
- Practitioner information
- Nature of the confidential relationship between counselor and client and a clear statement outlining exceptions to confidentiality
- Potential risks and benefits of treatment
- Alternatives to treatment
- Competence and lack of coercion
- Right to refuse or discontinue treatment without penalty
- Office hours, contact information, and what to do in the event of an emergency
- Fee structure and payment issues
- Privacy of private health information

141

Informed Consent and Minors

Minors cannot consent to their own treatment and practitioners must obtain consent from parents or legal guardians. For children who have been adjudicated dependent by a state court and are therefore in the custody of the state, the state's legal representative, usually an official from the state's Department of Children and Families or equivalent unit, is authorized to sign the consent for treatment. The rationale for requiring parental consent for the treatment of minors is the recognition of minors as a vulnerable group lacking full capacity to make informed decisions about their own care.

Assent to Treatment

An assent to treatment is a consent given by minors who have the capacity to have some meaningful understanding of the process of therapy that they are about to participate in. Although not legally obligatory, an assent to treatment by a minor involves the minor in a respectful way in making decisions about his or her own mental health care. Most sensitive and skilled practitioners already obtain assent for treatment from capable minors by discussing the process of counseling with them beforehand, answering any questions they may have including those concerning what kind of disclosures might be made to their parents, and by clearly describing the exceptions to confidentiality. Some practitioners develop a formal assent to treatment form for minors to parallel the consent to treatment form to be signed by their parents or legal guardians.

Involuntary Commitment and Informed Consent

In general, the procedure for involuntary commitment in most states includes a referral for involuntary commitment during which the person may be held for a relatively short time against their will in order that a psychiatric evaluation be conducted, and a hearing is held to determine if the patient should remain in the hospital. By definition, involuntary commitment eliminates the need for informed consent from the client or patient. By contrast, involuntary commitment increases the need for informed awareness of the heavy legal and ethical responsibilities incumbent on the referring mental health provider to follow a demonstrable standard of clinical judgment and demonstrable adherence to the clinical ethic of care for his client, including the duty to protect.

Online Counseling and Informed Consent

In October 1999, the Governing Council of the American Counseling Association approved their "Ethical Standards for Internet Online Counseling." These guidelines attempt to provide practitioners offering online counseling services with some basic standards for addressing issues of confidentiality, privacy of communications, client access to the counselor, and backup plans for handling online client emergencies. Because of the unique nature of the online counseling relationship, the process of informed consent must include all of the standard key elements but also must attend to online issues related to security of the Web sites and servers, expected turnaround time for counselor responses to client queries; determining the appropriateness of online counseling for a particular client; and providing backup professional help and referrals in the event of a client emergency. Additionally, the counselor must establish whether it is legal in his or her jurisdiction to provide online counseling to clients who may live in a state or states other than the one(s) in which the counselor is licensed.

Confidentiality–Final Considerations

In short, informed consent is a process that provides safeguards and benefits for both the client and counselor. However protective the process of informed consent may be for the counselor, it should be recognized primarily as a process for the promotion and enhancement of clients' well-being. At its best, the informed consent process is a relational one in which the counselor and client collaborate in a power sharing agreement that enhances trust in the counseling relationship and process. Informed consent rests on an ethic of care for the client from within which the counselor meticulously lays out all the details necessary for the client to have in order to make an informed decision about whether the particular counseling service offered is best for him or her. The counselor defers to the authority of the client's rights to self-agency and self-determination by providing an accurate and comprehensive informed consent procedure.

Guidelines for Insuring Informed Consent

- Know the ethics codes and legal statutes in your state or jurisdiction regarding informed consent. They typically specify the extent to which information can be disclosed and discussed with a client, as well as the conditions for disclosing information to other parties.
- Consider informed consent a process involving four parts rather than simply a single event. This can foster a relationship of trust and caring as well as reduce risk for the therapist. The four parts are: (1) client reads information outlining the elements of the informed consent document; (2) counselor ask if the client has any questions and then summarizes the intent of the document; (3) the client signs the document; and (4) because informed consent is an ongoing process the therapist informs the client of developments or options as treatment progresses.
- It is essential that this process of informed consent be documented. Thus, at or after the initial meeting with the client, a detailed intake note or report and a signed consent for agreement form is included in the client's file. Afterward, written notes should document any new developments or treatment options as counseling or therapy progresses.
- If one provides clinical supervision to trainees or others, informed consent for the process of supervision also should be secured.

INTERNET COUNSELING

It should not be too surprising that advancements in technology have prompted mental health practitioners to use technology, in particular the Internet, in providing professional services to clients. In response to this new method of service provision, the American Counseling Association, the American Psychological Association, the National Board for Certified Counselors, and the International Society for Mental Health Online, and others, have established guidelines for Internet practitioners. Because communicating online is becoming more prevalent, practitioners need to be aware of the legal and ethical issues and therapeutic concerns surrounding Internet counseling. The responsible use of Internet counseling requires that mental health practitioners implement specific technical safeguards in utilizing this new practice mode.

Terms and Related Considerations

Internet Counseling
Involves asynchronous and synchronous distance interaction among practitioners and clients using e-mail, chat, and videoconferencing features on the Internet to communicate. Also referred to as: web counseling, computer-mediated counseling, cybercounseling, e-counseling, e-mail-counseling, online counseling, and telehealth services.

Technology
The use of computers, tools, and other technical devices, and power for the purpose of production. It can be advanced or high-tech, that is, highly automated and specialized or low-tech, that is, labor-intensive and unspecialized.

Technical Safeguards
Safeguards required by HIPAA that require the creation and implementation of policies and procedures to protect from unauthorized access, alteration, or destruction of electronic protected health information. For example, a facility may employ software that can protect against viruses or corruption to protect client information.

Health Insurance Portability and Accountability Act (HIPAA)
The federal law designed to protect clients' privacy related to their medical information. It standardizes procedures across the United States for insuring the privacy and confidentiality of protected health information, including counseling and psychotherapy information.

Informed Consent
The client's right to base their decision about participating in counseling or therapy services—which includes assessment and interventions—after such services have been adequately described and explained in a manner that is understandable to the client. Information about the proposed services should include the purpose, risks and benefits, and possible alternative treatments, including the option of no treatment, as well an adequate description of exceptions to confidentiality and, where appropriate, what kind of reporting is required for court-ordered or mandatorily referred clients.

145

Confidentiality

The obligation of practitioners or therapists to respect the privacy of clients by not revealing to others the information communicated to them by clients during counseling sessions. In couples and family therapy, it is granted primarily to the whole (e.g., family) rather than to the individual, unless otherwise stated.

Potential Benefits and Risks of Internet Counseling

Potential Benefits

Internet counseling has significant potential for individuals who might not otherwise seek counseling to assist them with their problems. It can provide access to professional service for individuals in remote areas as well as for individuals whose medical conditions makes face-to-face contact with a professional difficult. Through Internet counseling, clients can send and receive messages at any time and can avoid the frustrations of "phone tag" and voice mail. Furthermore, Internet counseling allows clients to feel less inhibited than they would in person. Finally, clients can take their time in composing their messages, can reflect on responses to their messages, and keep a record of their communications to refer to later.

Potential Risks

A notable risk of Internet counseling is the lack of theoretical models for practice and the absence of solid research that affirms its quality or the circumstances under which Internet counseling can be used responsibly. Furthermore, the international nature of Web communications raises legal questions about jurisdiction regarding professional licensure in another country or state, and restricts the usual avenues of legal redress of consumers who feel poorly served. Internet counseling has the potential for several unique risks such as compromises to confidentiality of communications through e-mail and chat rooms, technical failures or delays that interrupt or terminate service, difficulties in verifying the identity of either party in the interaction, and problems in dealing with clients who are a danger to self or others.

Guidelines for Internet Counseling

Legal and Ethical Considerations

- Review pertinent legal and ethical codes for guidance on the practice of Internet counseling and supervision.
- Provide actual and potential clients with Internet links to Web sites of all appropriate certification bodies and licensure boards to facilitate consumer protection.
- Inform actual and potential clients that the practitioner's liability insurance provides coverage for Internet counseling services.
- Professional practitioners seek appropriate legal and technical assistance in the development and implementation of their Internet counseling services.

The Therapeutic Relationship

- Develop an appropriate in-take procedure for potential clients to determine whether Internet counseling is appropriate for the needs of the client.
- Develop individual Internet-counseling plans that are consistent with both the client's individual circumstances and the limitation of Internet counseling. Reach a mutual agreement on the frequency and the mode of communication, the method for determining the fee, the estimated cost to the client, and so on.
- Provide clients with a schedule of times during which the Internet counseling services will be available, including reasonable anticipated response times, and provide clients with an alternate means of contacting the professional counselor at other time.
- Provide services in areas within the practitioner's scope of competence, and should meet any necessary requirements to provide mental health services where he or she is located.
- Obtain the name and telephone number of a qualified local mental health care provider who has agreed to respond to the client in the case of an emergency, or a local crisis hotline or emergency number to provide to the client.
- Explain to the client the possibility of technical failure and discuss alternative modes of communication if a failure occurs, and how to cope with possible misunderstandings when visual cues do not exist.

147

- Make clients aware of free public access points to the Internet within the community for Internet counseling uses.
- Be aware that some clients may communicate in different languages, live in different time zones, have unique cultural perspectives, and that such local conditions and events may impact the client.

Informed Consent and Confidentiality

- Inform clients about the process, the practitioner, the potential risks and benefits of those services, safeguards against those risks, and alternatives to those services.
- Require clients to execute a client waiver agreement regarding acknowledgment of confidentiality procedures and risks.
- Determine if a client is a minor and therefore in need of parental/guardian consent.
- To protect confidentiality, steps should be taken to address imposter concerns, such as by using code words or numbers.
- Inform clients of encryption methods being used to help insure the security of client/counselor communications.
- Inform clients if, how, and how long session data are being preserved.
- Follow appropriate procedures regarding the release of information for sharing Internet client informational with other electronic sources.

ORGANIZATIONAL ETHICS

Organizational ethics reflect the organizational dynamics that can powerfully impact the professional and ethical decision making of professions within organizational contexts. Although organizational ethics does not replace personal, professional, or business ethics, it significantly expands the ethical perspective to include organizational factors and dynamics. Accordingly, effective and ethically sensitive therapists as well as school, clinic, or agency administrators would do well to become conversant with the organizational ethics dimension. Recognizing and understanding these dynamics is essential in making specific informed ethical decisions, as well as in evaluating the "fit" between an individual professional and the organization in which he or she is in training or works. A poor "fit" between personal and organizational values and practices can be distressing. An investigation of such organizational ethics and practices can

148

provide a plan for reducing one's stress by modifying those practices or even changing jobs or training site.

Terms and Related Considerations

Organizational Dynamics

An organization and its dynamics can be imaged as a set of five over-lapping, concentric circles representing the subsystems of structure, culture, strategy, leaders, and workers within a larger circle that represents the organization's external environment (Sperry, 1996; 2003). It should be noted that each of these six subsystems can influence ethical decisions.

Organizational Ethics

The form of ethics that recognizes the impact of organizational factors and involves the intentional use of values to guide decision making in organizational systems. Unlike business ethics and professional ethics that characteristically view a given ethical concern from an individual perspective, organizational ethics views the same ethical concerns from a systems perspective.

Professional Ethics

The form of ethics that endeavors to help professionals decide what to do when they are confronted with a case or situation that raise a ethical question or moral problem; it considers the morality of one's professional choices and is informed by a code and standards of ethics specified by one's profession.

Ethical Climate

The dimension of organizational culture that reflects the shared perceptions that staff and colleagues hold concerning ethical procedures and practices occurring with an organization.

Ethics Audit

An audit or investigation in which the implementation of ethical policies as well as ethical incidents in an organizational setting are reviewed and evaluated.

Organizational Ethics and Efficiency

For an organization to be successful, its ethical infrastructure must be aligned with its strategy and core values. Interestingly, ethical behavior has been shown to reflect such an alignment. When such alignment is not present "unethical behavior has been identified as a leading cause of operational inefficiency and poor quality" (Bottorff, 1997, p. 59). Accordingly, an organizational ethics strategy should "foster a virtuous organization whose ethical principles inspire appropriate decision making and moral behavior among its personnel" (Magill & Prybil, 2004, p. 227). Although surprising to many, research findings are clear: ethical organizations are more successful than unethical organizations (Verchsoor, 2003). Research evidence is mounting that the success of ethical organizations is reflected in several indices of performance. More specifically, ethical organizations have shown to have lower employee turnover rates, higher employee retention rates, higher quality of services, and higher levels of innovation. Furthermore, when the organization is a for-profit corporation, those organizations also have higher profitability (Magill & Prybil, 2004).

Mental Health and Counseling Organizations

Organizations including mental health clinics, human services agencies, and schools are well advised to consider ethics as important as counseling outcomes, quality services, trainee achievement, and legal and financial considerations. The administrators of such organizations must convey moral integrity, encourage ethical sensitivity, and support and reinforce ethical behavior. They support ethical behavior by upholding the organization's ethical values, requiring compliance with professional ethical standards, and by fostering a high degree of fit between personal values of staff and core values of the organization. Among other things, this means hiring staff with ethical sensitivity and competence.

Unethical Behaviors and Organizations

Nash identifies four systemic factors or organizational dynamics that appear to be major contributing causes to unethical organizational behaviors. They are: (1) the inarguable importance of the bottom line; (2) an overemphasis on short-term efficiency or expediency; (3) the seductive power of ego incentives; and (4) the difficulties of personally representing the organization's policies, that is, wearing two hats, that of a professional working and representing a particular organization and its values—organizational hat, and your own values—personal hat—which may differ significantly. Such a discrepancy between the two hats can be a source of considerable job stress.

Organizations and Confidentiality

As with other aspects of the provider-client relationship, issues of confidentiality can accompany the use of outcomes assessment, monitoring, and management. Just as clients should be informed in writing the extent to which confidentiality will be maintained in terms of provider communications and written records, clients should be informed as to how data that they provide on clinical outcomes inventories will be held confidential. Clinics need to develop written policy and procedure language as to who has access to such information and how that information will be used. Because clinical outcomes data at the assessment level and the management level tends to be aggregate data confidentiality issues are somewhat limited. By contrast, at the monitoring level individual data and policies need to indicate specifically how providers and staff will safeguard such client data.

Organizations and Informed Consent

Informed consent is a rather broad and complex legal and ethical issue. In managed care organizations, issues of informed consent often have revolved around economic factors, that is, a managed care organization pressuring their staff not to inform clients about specialized or expensive treatments that they are not willing to pay for or reimburse. In short, they simply withhold information about specialized, expensive treatments, the antithesis of informed consent.

Personal-Organizational Ethical Conflicts

Every individual wears several hats in fulfilling his or her organizational duties as well as personal and family responsibilities. Clinic administrators and practitioners routinely assume the roles of superior, coach, friend, parent, spouse, and behavioral health care advocate. These individuals also embody personal values that may or may not match actual—as contrasted with stated or written—organizational values. Business problems arise when there is a conflict between the administrators' personal roles and values and organizational roles and values. Matters of personal conscience inevitably become involved. These individuals continually face internal conflicts between what they would do as loyal representatives of the corporation and what they as private individuals might think is the right thing to do. Such a conflict is known as the "two-hat" dilemma and the ethical and moral dissonance between the two can be stressful.

Guidelines Involving Organizational Ethics

- Increase your personal awareness of how organizational dynamics impact the culture and climate as well as the way ethical and legal matters are handled in your counseling setting, whether it be an agency, school, or private practice. Completing an ethics audit is one way of increasing such knowledge.
- Increase the awareness of your colleagues in your clinic, agency, or school. The decision by a staff to undertake an ethics audit is more likely to lead to organizational change than if you are the only professional in that organization who has become increasingly aware of ethical and moral dissonance. Advocating for and undertaking an organization-wide audit can serve to foster focused discussion on ethical considerations and the need for change.
- Based on your personal audit or an ethics audit of your organization, consider your professional options. For example, consider what changes in policy or procedure could reduce dissonance. What is the likelihood of making or advocating for such change?
- Consider what liability—if any—might be consequence of your effort to change the ethical climate by impacting structure and culture. If the ethical climate seems relatively unchangeable, what other options are possible: secure the support of others, report or whistle blow, search for another position, and so on?
- If you work with trainees who are seeking community sites for clinical supervision, you might discuss organizational ethics and the dynamics of the "two hat" dilemma and subsequently how to find sites that are compatible with their personal values.

RELIGION, SPIRITUALITY, AND ETHICS

Religion and spirituality are part of the relational-multicultural dimension of counseling. Practitioners are required to be sensitive to religious and spiritual issues influencing their clients. It seems that increasing numbers of adults and older adults are searching for ways of incorporating spirituality in their daily lives. Survey research indicates that 94% of Americans believe in God, 9 out of 10 pray, 97% believe their prayers are answered, and 2 out of 5 report having life-changing spiritual experiences. Thus, it should not be too surprising that clients expect practitioners to incorporate the spiritual dimension in treatment.

Terms and Related Considerations

Religion
The search for significance through the sacred, within the context of a shared belief system, that is, doctrines, and communal ritual practice, that is, liturgy or public worship.

Spirituality
That unsatisfiable, deepest desire within everyone, and the ways individuals deal with that desire: how they think, feel, act, and interact in their quest to satisfy this unsatisfiable desire; the transcendent aspect of life that gives a sense of meaning and purpose to our lives.

Spiritual Incorporation
Extent to which practitioners incorporate spiritual and religious issues and interventions in their practice. Four levels of incorporation can be described. The higher the level, the more the dimension is incorporated. Central to each level is the extent to which a spiritual assessment, processing of spiritual issues and referral or collaboration with a priest, minister, rabbi, or spiritual advisor.

Spiritual Sensitivity
The capacity to be aware of and to recognize the importance and/or influence of religious or spiritual beliefs, values, and other factors on another's life.

153

Spiritual Competence

The capability for awareness of religious and spiritual dynamics and values, for assessment, for intervention, for collaboration and referral to ministers and spiritual advisors.

Ethics

Activity that studies how choices were made or should be made. This contrasts with morality, which is the activity of making choices and of deciding, judging, justifying, and defending those actions or behaviors called morals. Thus, ethics is the study of morality, of moral behavior, of moral decision making, and how one leads a good life.

Professional and Personal Stance Regarding Religion and Spirituality

In terms of their professional lives, the main implication is that "usual and customary care" requires sensitivity to spiritual and religious factors in the clinical practice. In terms of their personal lives, it does not mean that practitioners are expected to change their basic beliefs or ideology about religion and the spiritual domain. More specifically, it means that practitioners can maintain their status as agnostics, atheists, or as nominal or very devout adherents to a specific faith or spiritual path.

Levels of Incorporation of Spiritual Dimension in Counseling Practice

Four levels of incorporation of the practitioner's incorporation of the religious and spiritual dimension in counseling practice can be described. The higher the level, the more the dimension is incorporated. Central to each level is the extent to which a spiritual assessment, processing of spiritual issues, and referral or collaboration with a priest, minister, rabbi, or spiritual advisor is involved.

I. None	No spiritual assessment
	No processing of spiritual issues
	No spiritual advisor, even if indicated
II. Limited	Spiritual assessment
	No or very brief, single processing of spiritual issues
	Referral to spiritual advisor if indicated
III. Moderate	Spiritual assessment
	Some processing of spiritual issues
	Collaboration with a spiritual advisor if indicated
IV. Maximum	Spiritual assessment
	Full processing of spiritual issues
	Collaboration with a spiritual advisor is indicated

Spiritual Assessment

Eliciting a religious history or a spiritual assessment, as it is currently being called, is now considered an essential component of an initial evaluation. Although there is no standardized format or protocol for such an assessment, the following are four questions that are quite useful in eliciting key information:

1. "Is religion or spirituality important to you?"
2. "Do your religious or spiritual beliefs influence the way you look at your problems and the way you think about your health?"
3. "Would you like me to address your religious or spiritual beliefs and practices with you?"
4. "Are you part of a religious or spiritual community?"

Guidelines for Spiritual Sensitivity and Competence

Spiritual Sensitivity and Competencies—Involving the Counselor

- Explain relationship among the spiritual, religious, and transpersonal dimensions.
- Describes one's spiritual, religious, and transpersonal beliefs and practices.
- Identify key life events and how they contributed to one's spiritual/religious beliefs.

155

Spiritual Sensitivity and Competencies—Involving the Client

- Demonstrate empathy regarding the clients' spiritual or religious beliefs and practices.
- Acquire knowledge to better understand client's spiritual worldview.
- Assess the relevance of spiritual or religious issues regarding therapeutic goals.
- Identify when the counselor's understanding or tolerance of spiritual, religious, and transpersonal issues is inadequate to serve the client.
- Seek consultation and/or further education when indicated.
- Refer to minister, chaplain, rabbi, or other spiritual leader when indicated.

*Adapted from Association for Spiritual, Ethical and Religious Values in Counseling (Favier, Ingersoll, O'Brien and McNally, 2001, pp. 178–180).

TECHNOLOGY AND ETHICS

Recent technological advances have profoundly influenced the lives of every individual in terms of how one lives, works, and learns. Not surprisingly, technological advances have impacted mental health practice particularly in the way services are provided. Responsible practitioners need to recognize the impact of technology on their practice as well as understand the ethical and legal issues associated with these technological advances.

Terms and Related Considerations

Technology
The use of computers, tools and other technical devices, and power for the purpose of production. It can be advanced or high-tech, that is, highly automated and specialized or low-tech, that is, labor-intensive and unspecialized.

Technoanxious
Term referring to discomfort with computer technology, and is marked by fear and an attitude of avoidance of computerization of a profession.

Technocentered
Term referring to comfort and confidence in utilizing computer technology.

Health Insurance Portability and Accountability Act (HIPAA)
The federal law designed to protect clients' privacy related to their medical information. It standardizes procedures across the United States for ensuring the privacy and confidentiality of protected health information, including counseling and psychotherapy information.

Technical Safeguards
Safeguards required by HIPAA that require the creation and implementation of policies and procedures to protect from unauthorized access, alteration or destruction of electronic protected health information. For example, a facility may employ software that can protect against viruses or corruption to protect client information.

Internet Counseling
Internet counseling involves asynchronous and synchronous distance interaction among practitioners and clients using e-mail, chat, and videoconferencing features on the Internet to communicate. Also referred to as: WebCounseling, computer-mediated counseling, cyber-counseling, E-counseling, e-mail-counseling, online counseling, and telehealth services.

Legal and Ethical Implications of Technology

Technology has impacted mental health practice in various ways. Initially, technology improved efficiency of running the practitioner's practice. Photocopiers, fax machines, computers with word processing programs, voice mail, answering machines, and electronic claim submissions have not only increased efficiency and productivity but also have enabled practitioners to be more responsive in meeting clients' needs. More recent technological advancements such as computerized test administration, scoring, and interpretation, and telephone contact with clients between regularly scheduled sessions has further enhanced the provision of professional services. The most recent advances include Internet counseling and virtual reality methods in treating anxiety disorders. All of these advances have complicated various ethical and legal considerations involving confidentiality, informed consent, practitioner competency, and require compliance with professional ethical codes, legal statues, as well as the technical safeguards specified by HIPAA.

Guidelines for Ethically Utilizing
Technology in Professional Practice

Computers

- Utilize password protection or encryption for all confidential client information.
- Limit access to your computer and ensure that staff with access is trained in relevant ethical standards for confidentiality.
- Back up all computer data on disks and be sure that they are stored under lock and key.
- Utilize firewalls to prevent unauthorized access to confidential materials on the Internet.

Fax Machines

- Ascertain who has access to the receiving fax machine before sending faxes.
- Utilize a cover sheet that clearly identifies the transmission as confidential and provides instructions for those who may receive it in error.

Cell Phones

- Recognize that certain frequencies of cellular communications may be accessed by some AM radios and nursery monitors.
- Refrain from discussing confidential material with identifying information during such calls.

Photocopying Machines

- Shred or otherwise destroy all patient records and other materials with confidential information that are photocopied and need to be discarded. Merely throwing away discarded photocopies in the trash is a threat to client confidentiality.

Answering Machines and Voicemail

- Ascertain the extent to which the client's voicemail is private. When others have access to it, only leave minimal information that in no way compromises confidentiality, such as your identity as a mental health practitioner.

- When playing back messages on your answering machine, be sure to do so in private so that confidential information is not inadvertently disclosed.

Internet Counseling

- Utilize an informed consent procedure that is tailored to Internet counseling; obtain appropriate consent before providing online services.
- Know relevant Internet counseling laws for all jurisdictions in which you will be providing online services before the services are provided.
- Follow all applicable professional standards and the ethics code of your profession, regardless of the medium used or the type of services provided.
- Ensure client confidentiality, using encryption and other technologies whenever possible. However, also be aware of necessary breaches of confidentiality and attend to issues of dangerousness, duty to warn and protect situations, and mandatory reporting requirements.
- Arrange for coverage of emergency and crisis situations that may arise in the client's local area.
- Ensure the accuracy of advertising and public statements about online services offered and ensure that these statements do not imply a level of treatment or effectiveness that is not actually provided.
- Maintain adequate liability coverage and be sure that malpractice insurance covers online services provided.
- Remain aware of the limitations of both the online services and the technology used to offer them.

[Refer to the section titled "Internet Counseling" (p. 144) for a fuller discussion of the issue and guidelines for enhancing ethical and legal practice.]

USING CASE MATERIAL IN PRESENTATIONS AND PUBLICATIONS

Preparing clinical case material for presentation or publication is a common expectation for practitioners. Often, the case material is for a formal case conference or a clinical illustration in a course, workshop, or other type of presentation. An increasing concern for those publishing in professional journals and books is how a practitioner can describe clients in a case illustration without changing their personal qualities so much that the client's disguise vitiates the point of the illustration. Whatever the situation, practitioners are faced with the essential ethical consideration of protecting client confidentiality. Ensuring confidentiality effectively means modifying or disguising the case material. What is the extent and type of changes or disguises needed to ensure confidentiality? How can practitioners prepare case material that adequately maintains such confidentiality? Is it sufficient, necessary, and appropriate to disguise gender, for example, making a male client female or an elderly client a middle age one, to just limit identifying information, or is it better to present a composite case? These considerations and some guidelines are addressed in the following paragraphs.

Terms and Related Considerations

Disguising Case Material
A method of modifying clinical case material for presentation or publication that endeavors to protect client confidentiality. There are various methods and strategies that can be employed to ensure that a given client's identity is difficult or impossible for others to detect. These include altering, limiting, and observing case material.

Alteration of Specific Characteristics
The most common method of disguising material was alteration of specific characteristics. Changing demographics factors such as occupation, employment, age, and geographic locale were most commonly cited changes. Other common changes included parental information, ethnicity, and number of children. Case information that the respondents believed should *not* be altered included presenting problem, gender, psychological test data, reported feeling, reported thoughts, and reported behaviors.

Limiting Description of Specific Characteristics
The next most common was limiting a description of specific characteristics. The most frequent method was deleting uniquely personal and professional information that could conceivably identify the client. Another frequent limiting method was to significantly limit the number of client or case identifiers. Limiting such case descriptors is particularly appropriate when the presented or published case emphasizes the application of a

particular clinical intervention rather than illustrating an assessment or diagnostic method.

Obscuring the Case Description

The least frequent method was that of obfuscating or obscuring the case description by adding extraneous material. The basic obscuring strategy was to develop a composite case illustration based on two or more case studies. Intuitively, this strategy seems to be the most likely to ensure confidentiality. Unfortunately, composite cases can be quite difficult to create while maintaining the point or points of the case that one wants to illustrate.

Developing Case Material for Presentations and Publications

In a study undertaken by the Publication and Communication Board of the American Psychological Association, a survey of senior authors with multiple publications found that these authors utilized one or more of three disguise strategies: altering the description of specific characteristics, limiting description of specific characteristics, and obscuring the case description (defined earlier). Other data from the APA study is worth noting. Of particular interest and practical significance is the fact that the authors surveyed disguised an average of 3.69 factors or elements of a particular clinical case when they were preparing a clinical case for publication. Furthermore, they also reported that they changed an average of 6.12 case variables in a case study in at least one case that they had published sometime in their career. Interestingly, and consistent with the APA survey, a rule of thumb that some professional book publisher and journal editors have adopted is that authors are expected to disguise at least three to four identifying factors in a case illustration.

Although there may be some differences between case material prepared for publication versus live presentation, there are many similarities. It may well be that disguising three to four client identifying factors is a reasonable rule of thumb for practitioners preparing case material for a presentation.

Finally, it should be noted that there are circumstances in which case material does not have to be disguised for presentation of case material. These exceptions are noted in the guidelines that follow.

Guidelines for Disguising Case Material

- Disguising case material is not necessary when you have your client's explicit written authorization. Specifically, this means having the client sign a specific authorization for you to disclose information about the case in a given presentation at a professional meeting. There also is language in the initial informed consent agreement with the client that should specify the circumstances in which case material may be discussed with others such as with a supervisor or case consultant, an in-house staffing, or a case conference.
- Disguising case material is necessary to protect client confidentiality when you do not have explicit authorization from your client to do so in a forum such as a publication or a presentation outside the initial informed consent agreement with the client.
- Currently, alteration of three to four specific case descriptors is considered sufficient for adequately disguising and safeguarding confidentiality. The most commonly altered demographics factors include occupation, employment, age, and geographic locale. Obviously, if you are known by your audience to work only with a certain age range of clients or have practiced exclusively in only one geographical area, the option of changing age or geographical locale is not viable to maintain credibility with your audience and so other disguising factors should be substituted.
- Generally speaking, case information such as presenting problem, gender, psychological test data, and reported client feeling, thoughts, and behaviors should not be altered.
- The method obscuring the case description by adding extraneous material or by developing a composite case is quite challenging and time consuming, so it probably should be reserved for those rare instances when altering or limiting descriptive factors cannot adequately disguise or will distort case material.

Part III

Legal Issues and Considerations

Colette L. Corcoran, J.D., L.M.H.C., and Len Sperry, M.D., Ph.D.

Mental health professionals regularly face professional situations involving legal issues and considerations. This handbook is intended to be a "ready reference" for the most common legal issues and considerations professional face in everyday practice. Part III has been designed to provide you with key points about such issues and considerations. It describes each issue or consideration directly and concisely. Because legal language tends to be rather technical and arcane, we have endeavored to make Part III as user-friendly as possible. To save you the time and effort of looking up specific terms in the Dictionary section of this book, we have included definitions of key terms relevant to each topic right in the discussion of each legal issue or consideration. Clinical applications of each topic are described and guidelines are presented. The following legal issues and considerations are discussed in this section.

- ABCs of Legal Theory and Reasoning
- Americans with Disabilities Act (ADA)
- Billing and Fees
- Bartering

- Child Custody
- Client Complaints
- Competency (Client)
- Confidentiality, Limits to
- Conflicts of Interest
- Depositions
- Diminished Capacity
- Duties to Third Parties
- Duty to Warn and Duty to Protect
- End-of-Life Considerations
- Expert Testimony I: General Considerations
- Expert Testimony II: *Frye* and *Daubert*
- Health Information Portability and Accountability Act (HIPAA)
- Liability in Supervision: Direct and Indirect
- Malpractice
- Mandatory Reporting
- Record Keeping
- Repressed and Recovered Memories
- Sexual Misconduct
- Subpoenas, Responding to
- Terminating Counseling /Therapy
- Testimonial Privilege

Readers might find it useful to refer to the first entry, "ABCs of Legal Theory and Reasoning," to become more familiar with the way in which the courts and the legal profession think about and arrive at judgments or decisions. A common example illustrates the process of legal reasoning and distinguishes state versus federal rulings.

ABCS OF LEGAL THEORY AND REASONING

Legal theory and reasoning underlie state and federal statutes and case law governing how practitioners practice. The legislative branch of the government must have a specific reason to enact a statute, such as a criminal law enacted to protect society as a whole from wrongful actions, or a civil law enacted to help to solve problems that occur between individuals or groups. Courts often are called on to interpret the laws and statutes created by the legislative branch, and the opinions written by the court is called case law. Courts often will refer to the legislative intent in creating statutes or rules in determining how to interpret them and the rationale will be articulated in the form of a legal opinion.

Example of Legal Theory and Reasoning in Action: *Tarasoff* Decision

The law, including statutes, rules, and case law, is ever-changing and constantly evolving to meet the needs of the people. For example, in the California *Tarasoff* case, Prosenjit Poddar, a client in therapy, made a threat against Tatiana Tarasoff, a woman who had rebuffed him romantically, to his psychotherapist. The psychotherapist attempted unsuccessfully to have Mr. Poddar involuntarily committed and Mr. Poddar discontinued therapy. Two months after Mr. Poddar's disclosure to his psychotherapist of his threat to harm Ms. Tarasoff, Mr. Poddar actually murdered Ms. Tarasoff. Tatiana Tarasoff's parents brought suit against the University of California and its employees on the grounds of failure to commit Mr. Poddar and the failure to warn Ms. Tarasoff of the danger. The suit fueled a national debate about the limits of confidentiality and injuries arising out of nonaction. The Tarasoff case was actually determined twice.

The initial decision in 1974, *Tarasoff v. Regents of University of Cal.*, 13 Cal. 3d 177 (1974), assessed liability for the failure of the psychotherapist to *warn* Ms. Tarasoff of the danger to her. The 1974 decision essentially created a duty to warn and sparked so much controversy that the California Supreme Court actually decided to re-review the case.

The subsequent decision in 1976, *Tarasoff v. Regents of the University of California*, 551 P.2d 334, 345 (Cal. 1976), modified the rationale of the 1974 decision and assessed liability based on the failure to *protect* Ms. Tarasoff from the danger to her. The 1976 decision set the stage for a series of groundbreaking cases that held that once a psychotherapist determines or reasonably should have determined that a client poses a serious danger of violence to others, the psychotherapist bears a duty to exercise reasonable care to protect the foreseeable victim of that danger, notwithstanding confidentiality and the general rule at common law that one person owes neither a duty to control the conduct of another nor a duty to warn those endangered by such conduct. The 1976 decision was based primarily on the affirmative duty to act that arises out of the "special relationship" between a psychotherapist and a patient. The State of California legislature later codified the *Tarasoff* decision.

Court rulings following the *Tarasoff* decision, in California and many other states, have adopted, clarified, and, to some extent, limited the violation of client confidentiality only when the client states an intent to harm a specific intended victim. Generally, as a direct offshoot of the *Tarasoff* case, when a client states an intent to harm a specific victim, practitioners must attempt to contact both the intended victim and local law enforcement to fully comply with the duty to warn and duty to protect. Although the practitioner duty to warn and protect has yet to become a federal matter, most states, either by statute, rule, or case law, and professional organizations, by ethical guidelines, have created a duty to warn and duty to protect.

State versus Federal Rulings

Finally, it is noteworthy that Tarasoff has not become the law of the land. *Jaffe v. Redmond* was the landmark case establishing psychotherapist-client privilege. Although the Tarasoff case was decided by the California Supreme Court and then enacted into law by various state legislatures, the *Jaffe v. Redmond* decision was handed down by the U.S. Supreme Court to make psychotherapist-client privilege applicable in all states and jurisdictions.

AMERICANS WITH DISABILITIES ACT (ADA)

The Americans with Disabilities Act, 42 USCS §12101 (2005) (ADA), is a federal civil right law that was passed in 1990. The ADA is a comprehensive law that prohibits discrimination against certain qualified persons with disabilities. The legislation specifically states, "No individual shall be discriminated against on the basis of a disability in the full and equal enjoyment of the goods, services, facilities, privileges, advantages or accommodations of any place of public accommodation by any person who owns, leases or operates a place of public accommodation." One rationale for the enactment of the legislation was that approximately 43 million Americans had one or more physical or mental disabilities, and this number is increasing as the population as a whole is growing older. Additionally, historically, society has tended to isolate and segregate individuals with disabilities, and, despite some improvements, such forms of discrimination against individuals with disabilities were a serious and pervasive social problem.

The ADA prohibits entities covered by the law from discriminating against a qualified person with a disability in employment (Title I), governmental services (Title II), public accommodations (Title III), and telecommunications (Title IV). Title III of the ADA is the most likely to impact practitioners. Title III prohibits discrimination by private entities and nonprofit service providers operating public accommodations and mandates that public accommodations not exclude, segregate, or treat people with disabilities unequally. Compliance with Title III requires that each entity meet the architectural standards for providing physical access, reasonable modifications to policies, practices and procedures, effective communication with people with disabilities and other various access requirements. Additionally, public accommodations must remove barriers in existing structures where it would not be difficult to do so considering the public accommodation's resources. Enforcement of public accommodations of Title III of the ADA is the responsibility of the Civil Rights Division of the U.S. Department of Justice.

Title I, which is less frequently a concern for practitioners, requires employers with 15 or more employees to provide qualified individuals with disabilities an equal opportunity to benefit from the full range of employment-related opportunities available to others. Title I complaints must be filed with the U.S. Equal Employment Opportunity Commission.

It is important to note that the ADA provides the minimum standard through which people with disabilities are protected. Each state has the ability to enact legislation, which heightens the protections for those already protected by the ADA. The states cannot, however, require less than that mandated by the ADA.

Terms and Related Considerations

Americans with Disabilities Act (ADA)
Federal legislation enacted in 1990 that bars employers from discriminating against disabled persons in hiring, promotion, or other provisions of employment, especially in the provision of reasonable accommodation in response to their disability.

Disability
An identifiable physical or mental condition whose functional limitations, when manifested, are recognized and may be overcome with appropriate accommodations.

Impairment
The incapacity to perform specific functions because of a debilitating medical, substance-related, or psychological condition, which results in diminished functioning from a previous higher level of functioning.

Reasonable Accommodation
Any modification or adjustment to a job or the work environment that will enable a qualified applicant or employee with a disability to participate in the application process or to perform essential job functions. It also includes adjustments to assure that a qualified individual with a disability has rights and privileges in employment equal to those of employees without disabilities.

Qualified Persons with a Disability under Title III of ADA
Three specific groups of people receive protection under the ADA. The first group is comprised of people with a physical or mental impairment that substantially limits one or more major life activities. The second group is comprised of people with a history of a physical or mental impairment that substantially limits one or more major life activities. Finally, the third group is comprised of people who are regarded as having a physical or mental impairment that substantially limits one or more major life activities.

Private Entities Operating Public Accommodations under Title III of ADA
With some exceptions, private entities operating public accommodations are private entities that own, lease, lease to, or operate facilities open to the public. Some examples include restaurants, retail stores, hotels, movie theaters, private schools, convention centers, doctors' offices, homeless shelters, transportation depots, zoos, funeral homes, day care centers, recreation facilities including sports stadiums and fitness clubs, and other commercial facilities. Private clubs and religious organizations are exempt.

Purposes of the ADA

The following are the four legislatively stated purposes of the ADA:

1. to provide a clear and comprehensive national mandate for the elimination of discrimination against individuals with disabilities;
2. to provide clear, strong, consistent, enforceable standards addressing discrimination against individuals with disabilities;
3. to ensure that the federal government plays a central role in enforcing the standards established in this Act on behalf of individuals with disabilities; and
4. to invoke the sweep of congressional authority, including the power to enforce the 14th amendment and to regulate commerce, in order to address the major areas of discrimination faced day-to-day by people with disabilities.

Title III of the ADA Violations

Complaints of violations of Title III of the ADA may be filed with the U.S. Department of Justice. The Department of Justice is authorized to bring a lawsuit where there is a pattern or practice of discrimination in violation of Title III, or where an act of discrimination raises an issue of general public importance. It is not necessary, however, to pursue a complaint with the U.S. Department of Justice. An individual or group of individuals may also sue a private entity operating public accommodations for a violation of Title III of ADA through private lawsuits. Such lawsuits may be extremely costly and emotionally tolling to the individual or entity being sued.

Guidelines for Complying with the Americans with Disabilities Act

- Practitioners should review the ADA in full. A copy of the ADA is available from the U.S. Department of Justice.
- Practitioners must not exclude, segregate, or treat individuals with disabilities unequally.
- Practitioners are advised to review the ADA Standards for Accessible Design regarding architectural standards for providing physical access, and make all reasonable accommodations. A copy of the ADA Standards for Accessible Design is also available from the U.S. Department of Justice.

- Practitioners should make all reasonable modifications to policies, practices, and procedures to be fully compliant with the ADA.
- If employed by an entity covered by the ADA, practitioners should encourage your employer to comply with the ADA.
- If necessary, practitioners should consult an attorney, to ensure compliance with the Americans with Disabilities Act.

BILLING AND FEES

Beginning practitioners often find establishing fees for services and billing practices particularly challenging and uncomfortable. It is important that the clinic or practitioner's fee structure, expectations for the method and timing of compensation, and policy regarding missed sessions, are established at the outset of treatment and are ideally addressed during the informed consent process. If handled inappropriately, the practitioner could hinder the therapeutic relationship and may even be subject to civil or criminal penalties. Some clients pay for mental health services out of pocket and benevolent practitioners may want to apply a sliding fee scale or reduced rate, which could be a dangerous venture for the practitioner. Other clients may pay through a third party such as an insurance company or managed care organization. Specific issues arise therewith, all of which also should be clearly addressed at the outset of treatment, with the client having a clear understanding regarding copayments, expected length of insurance coverage, confidentiality, assignment of benefits, and termination of coverage by the insurer. Finally, the collection of unpaid fees or copayments must be handled in accordance with legal and ethical guidelines to promote the client's well-being while still protecting the practitioner from liability.

Billing and Fees and Related Considerations

Billing
The practice by which the practitioner informs the client and third party payor, if applicable, on an ongoing basis of the amount that is owed for services rendered and by whom.

Fees
The amount of money charged for a certain time period with the practitioner or in some cases, for a particular service performed by the practitioner (i.e., an evaluation).

Copayment
The amount required by some insurers to be paid by the client to the practitioner in addition to that which is by the third-party payor or insurance company.

Establishing Fees and Financial Arrangements

Both the ACA and the NASW codes of ethics require that practitioners take into account the client's financial status in establishing a fee for services. Essentially, the fee must be reasonable in consideration of the client, the practitioner's experience, and the locality. It is possible for a practitioner to operate on a sliding-scale fee policy, where the amount the clients pay depends on income; however, it is never appropriate for a practitioner to charge a higher rate for those clients with insurance coverage solely because they have insurance. Because of the proliferation of litigation against practitioners for assessing variable fees for services resulting in higher rates for clients who have insurance, it appears that practitioners must either establish a uniform rate for services or adopt a sliding scale that is applied consistently for all clients.

Third-Party Payors

Many insurance companies, including HMOs and other types of managed care plans, and employee assistance programs provide coverage or partial coverage for mental health services. Because insurance companies or health maintenance organizations exert a great deal of force over both the counseling process and the length of treatment, as soon as practicable practitioners should find out how much the insurance company will reimburse for mental health services and what limitations on the use of benefits may apply and relay that information to the client. A significant concern for many clients is the requests of the insurance company for the personal information about the client. In general, insurance companies will not cover mental health services without confidential client information and there is always a tension between the client's confidentiality and

171

the insurance company's need for information to determine qualifications for treatment. Practitioners are required to obtain written consent from the client before releasing any confidential information about a client to an insurance company.

The number of cases wherein the practitioner provides the service to the client without remuneration at the time of service because there is an expectation that the insurance company will pay the fees, the practitioner bills the insurance company, the insurance company sends the payment to the client, has increased. The practitioner then has to recover the payment from the client. Before providing services with the expectation of payment from an insurance company, practitioners should ensure that there is an assignment of benefits clause with the insurance company, meaning that the insurance company will direct payments to the treatment provider for services rendered to the insured. An alternative is for the practitioner to require the client to pay for each session and request reimbursement from the insurer for all funds spent.

Fees for Missed Appointments

When a client fails to notify a practitioner that an appointment will be missed, the practitioner has the right to require the client to pay for the missed session, as long as the client initially consented to this arrangement. Because most insurance companies have a policy that they will not pay for a missed appointment, if the practitioner plans to charge for missed sessions the client needs to be informed at the outset of treatment that the client will most likely be personally liable for the missed session fee if cancellation is not made within a specified period of time.

Collections

Client nonpayment of fees or copayments is a reality in counseling practice. Collections can be especially problematic with clients with certain personality disorders, such as paranoid, borderline, narcissistic, and passive aggressive personality disorders. The ethical codes of both the ACA and the APA obligate the practitioner to notify the clients of their intent to use collection agencies or take legal measures to collect unpaid fees or copayments and offer the client an opportunity to make payments toward the delinquent account. If the client fails to bring the account balance current, the practitioner may send the case to a collection agency or attorney for legal action; however, this usually is not preferred because it could hinder the well-being of the client by giving the client a problem in addition to that which he or she originally had at the outset of counseling (i.e., additional debt, interaction with a collections agency).

By contrast, it is both illegal and unethical not to attempt to collect a copayment from a client when the insurance company is paying a certain portion of the fee for services. For example, if the managed care company contracts with a practitioner that the fee is $90 per hour with a $10 copayment, the managed care company is agreeing to pay for 90% of that client's session. When the practitioner agrees with the client to "waive" the $10 copayment, the managed care company is actually paying for 100% of the fee that the practitioner is charging for the session rather than the originally agreed 90%. Consequently, the insurance company can initiate a legal action for fraud against the practitioner.

Withholding Records for Nonpayment

In cases of client emergency, a practitioner should never withhold medical records based on nonpayment of fees or copayments. Outside of emergencies, the matter regarding the withholding of medical records for nonpayment becomes murkier; however, the client's well-being should always be paramount.

Guidelines for Establishing Fees and Billing Practices

- Practitioners must establish the fee structure and the expectations for the method and timing of payment at the outset of treatment, during the informed consent process.
- In order to comply with the law, practitioners should adopt a uniform rate for services or adopt a sliding scale, which is applied consistently for all clients.
- Practitioners should make a good faith effort to collect all unpaid fees and copayments from clients directly before engaging a collection agency or lawyer.
- In all cases, practitioners must protect client confidentiality with regard to third-party payors by only disclosing information for which the client has consented and only so much as necessary.

- Practitioners should provide the client's medical record when requested by the client if it will promote the client's well-being notwithstanding the client's unpaid fees or copayments.
- Practitioners are advised to discontinue debt collection efforts once it becomes clear that a client will not pay.

BARTERING

Since the beginning of time, people have bartered goods and services. Although bartering counseling for the goods or services of a client is rarely seen in urban communities, it is much more common in rural areas. Among practitioners, bartering has been an especially controversial issue because, first, it is a dual relationship wherein the practitioner is engaging in more than one role with the client and, second, it is thought that there is a power disparity between the practitioner and the client that may lead to exploitation of the client by the practitioner in the bartering arrangement. Most ethics codes for professional associations address the issue of bartering and place numerous restrictions, if allowing it at all. The ethical codes usually warn that practitioners can only barter with a client at the client's request, if the practitioner is sure that the relationship is not exploitive or harmful to the client, and the barter does not place the practitioner in an unfair advantage. Another factor often considered is whether such arrangements are an accepted practice of professionals in that locality or community. Additionally, practitioners are urged to consider the cultural implications of bartering, such as whether it is customary in the client's culture to barter for services even where the client may not live in a rural community. At the outset of the barter arrangement, the practitioner must discuss the relevant concerns with clients and document such agreements in a clear written contract.

Bartering and Related Considerations

Bartering
The APA ethics code (2002) defines barter as the acceptance of goods, services, or other nonmonetary remuneration from clients in return for psychological services. The bartering of goods involves the exchange of a tangible item(s), such as artwork, cattle, or a chair, for counseling. In such cases, the value of the goods would be determined in a collaborative fash-

174

ion between the practitioner and the client and that determined value acts as a credit for counseling sessions. For instance, if the client offers to barter a lamp determined to be worth $300 and the practitioner's hourly rate is $100 per hour, there would be an exchange of three counseling sessions for the lamp. The bartering of services involves the exchange of the client's services for counseling and similar to bartering for goods, the value of the services would be determined in a collaborative fashion between the client and practitioner whether it is an hourly rate or flat fee for the client's services. For example, a landscaper who mows the practitioner's lawn for $25 per hour in exchange for counseling at a rate of $100 would have to mow the practitioner's lawn for four hours for each hour of counseling received.

Conflict of Interest

A conflict of interest arises when a practitioner has two or more competing interests with regard to a client that may impede the practitioner's ability to faithfully exercise his or her professional judgment and skill in working with that client.

Nonmaleficence

The moral principle of nonmalficence is the foundation to most of the helping professions and means to do no harm.

Legal and Ethical Aspects

Potential Benefits

The dual relationship of bartering can be either a complimentary or conflicting relationship. In a complimentary dual relationship, the client's well-being is enhanced as a result of being involved in both of the dual relationships. In rural communities, bartering may be the only way some people of lower socioeconomic status are able to receive counseling at all and clients in general take pride in paying for counseling sessions. In such situations, the expectation is that a complimentary relationship is established because the client receives the benefit of counseling and the satisfaction of knowing that there was compensation, whether goods or services, in exchange for counseling rather than receiving counseling as charity. Additionally, practitioners may engage in bartering purposely to enhance the client's well-being as part of a client's treatment plan and consequently, the client benefits as a result of engaging in both of the dual relationships and a complementary dual relationship is established.

Potential Risks

There is always a possibility that the power disparity between the practitioner and the client can lead to exploitation of the client by the practitioner in the bartering arrangement or that there is a conflict between the professional and nonprofessional (bartering) relationships that ultimately causes the loss of professional objectivity and harm to the client. Although there is a risk of client exploitation in deciding on the price when bartering goods for counseling, it is generally accepted that the risk for both the practitioner and the client increases when a practitioner barters for a client's services. For instance, if a client agrees to work at an hourly rate for the practitioner and the client has to work several hours in exchange for one counseling hour, the client could develop a resentment against the practitioner. By contrast, the client could incompetently or poorly perform the service that was agreed and the practitioner could harbor a resentment against the client.

Moreover, the type of service may be the deciding factor as to whether the bartering creates a complimentary or conflicting dual relationship. Perhaps house painting and automobile repairs are acceptable services in exchange for counseling in certain situations, especially in more rural areas; however, more intimate services such as massages or personal escort services in exchange for counseling are not acceptable practices. Obviously, there is a much higher risk for boundary violations when there is intimate contact between the client and the practitioner.

Another concern is that the client, as a result of the barter, may learn additional information about the practitioner about which the client would not have known but for the barter. For example, if the client cleans the practitioner's house as part of the barter, the client may learn intimate details about the practitioner that could hinder the client's ability to focus on therapy. Finally, there is also a concern that the practitioner may avoid paying income tax as a result of bartering counseling for goods or services because actual monetary compensation is not received.

Generally, the practitioner has the responsibility to be mindful of the power differential and ensure the client's well-being before agreeing to barter. The NASW ethics code (1999) even goes so far as to say that social workers who accept goods or services from clients as payment for professional services assume the full burden of demonstrating that this arrangement will not be detrimental to the client or the professional relationship.

Guidelines for Entering into a Bartering Agreement

- Practitioners are advised to review the code of ethics of the applicable professional association and/or state or federal laws about bartering.
- When necessary, practitioners must determine what ethical principle(s) guiding clinical behavior would be helpful in deciding whether to enter into a barter agreement.
- Practitioners need to survey whether such arrangements are an accepted practice of professionals in that locality.
- If bartering is commonplace in a particular practitioner's locality, the practitioner must ensure that the "Consent for Treatment" form contains a clear and detailed explanation of the bartering arrangement, specifying the exact terms including price of goods or services exchanged for counseling and length of time during which the bartering agreement will take place.
- Practitioners should continually evaluate the potential for exploitation, conflicts of interest, or harm to the client.
- Before beginning counseling, practitioners should confirm that the client involved understands the consequences and risks of bartering.
- Practitioners should take all measures necessary to protect the well-being of the client if a misunderstanding about the barter arises.
- As needed, practitioners should consult with a supervisor or consultant about whether a barter in a particular situation is appropriate.

CHILD CUSTODY

The ethical and legal issues that arise when a practitioner treats a minor child are challenging; however, the complexities increase exponentially when the minor child being treated or about to be treated is involved in a custody dispute. Practitioners involved in child custody disputes will usually take one of two roles. The first is that of the treating practitioner of the minor child or some member of the family and the second is that of the child custody evaluator. It is imperative that practitioners recognize that the role of child custody evaluator in a child custody dispute is dramatically different from that of a treating practitioner in a traditional setting. A practitioner who attempts to take both roles is potentially creating a dual relationship. Practitioners need to make it clear to the clients from the outset whether their role with the client shall be as an evaluating practitioner or as a treating practitioner. The client has the right to base his or her decision about participating in the relationship after the relationship or the services to be received are fully explained in a manner that is understandable to the client.

Sometimes it is unclear whether a practitioner witness is testifying as an expert witness or a fact witness and advocate for one side. Practitioners performing child custody evaluations should express well-balanced, objective opinions about the case and their experience with the parties. Treating practitioners have the liberty to act as an advocate for their clients and often are practitioners for one party who have had minimal, if any, contact with the other party. Because a treating practitioner cannot provide an objective evaluation, treating practitioners for one of the parties should not serve as an expert witness.

Child Custody and Related Considerations

Custody
Refers to the rights and responsibilities of parents with regard to their children. Legal custody involves the right and responsibility of the parent to make decisions about the child's life, while physical custody is the right and responsibility of the parent to reside with the child.

Custody Dispute
A disagreement between parents over the rights to their children.

Custody Evaluation
An examination of children's home environment and their relationships with their parents used by a court in awarding custody. Evaluators are typically court appointed mental health professionals who undertake such evaluations.

Custodial Parent
The divorced parent with whom the children live and who is typically the recipient of child support.

Expert
A person who, by virtue of training or experience, has developed specialized knowledge on a particular subject so that he or she is able to form an opinion that a person without such knowledge could not provide.

Testifying Expert
An expert who is identified by a party in litigation as a potential expert witness for trial.

Custody Evaluator Competence

It is critically important that custody evaluators are competent. Competence refers to a practitioner's capability to provide a minimum quality of service within the practitioner's scope of practice. Practitioners who are unfamiliar with the nuances of working with courts or the requirements for a custody evaluation would not be deemed competent to perform a custody evaluation. Generally, a practitioner performing custody evaluations should have concrete knowledge of his or her jurisdictions statutes and professional association guidelines about performing child custody evaluations, an engaging style when working with individuals, an appreciation of family relationships and interpersonal dynamics, an understanding for child and adult developmental issues, and familiarity with family law in the local jurisdiction.

Standards for Child Custody Evaluations

Currently, the "best interests of the child" is the prevailing legal standard used by courts for custody decisions. Although there are wide variations in how this concept is interpreted by judges, it generally favors the custody arrangement that best fulfills the needs of the specific children involved and fosters their normative development.

Guidelines for Addressing Child Custody Issues

- At the outset of the new relationship with a client, the practitioner must clarify himself or herself as a treating practitioner or an evaluating practitioner.

179

- When qualified as an expert regarding a child custody evaluation, the practitioner should testify in an objective and candid manner, regardless of which party retained him or her.
- Practitioners are advised to stay current with the field through conferences, continuing education, seeking diplomate status, consulting with colleagues, and reading journals, guidelines, and other publications.
- Practitioners should consult all data available about the case.
- When practitioners give an expert opinion or conduct an assessment, the practitioner should base the evaluation only on the data available.
- It is recommended that practitioners address the limitations of custody evaluation and make statements about the certainty of findings. For example, if no interview of one of the parents was possible, note the limitations in the report.
- Where the facts are disputed, it is possible for the practitioner to explain the contradictions between the information received from the two parties and prepare a set of recommendations for each plausible scenario, allowing the court to decide which party is truthful.
- At all times during a deposition or courtroom testimony, practitioners must remain calm, cool, and collected.
- Practitioners must always tell the truth.

CLIENT COMPLAINTS: HOW BOARDS AND PROFESSIONAL ORGANIZATIONS RESPOND

Clients expect that practitioners are competent professionals. When a client perceives that his or her expectations were not met, he or she may complain to the practitioner or file a complaint against the practitioner with a professional organization, certification board, or licensing board. Licensure, certification, and membership in professional organizations all provide a mechanism through which there is a stated minimum standard of service to the public in order to monitor and discipline practitioners when necessary. It is important to note that a client must waive his or her right to confidentiality in order to file a complaint against the practitioner. In general, on receipt of a client complaint, a professional organization or licensing board will evaluate the client complaint to determine whether probable cause exists to investigate further and, if so, will investigate the possible code, rule, or statutory violations, and, if necessary, will apply disciplinary action in cases involving the misconduct of a practitioner.

Licenses and credentials do not always ensure that practitioners will competently do that which their license or credential permits. When they do not, the practitioner may be held accountable and the client may have some recourse. For practitioners, competence is the best defense against client complaints.

Client Complaints and Related Considerations

Membership
Membership in a professional organization such as the American Counseling Association or the American Psychological Association is usually voluntary and represents to the public that the person holding the membership wishes to use the title of "member" to perform services and is expected, when practicable and in some cases as permitted by law, to follow that professional organization's code of ethics.

Certification
Certification, which may be issued by the state or an independent organization such as the National Board of Certified Counselors, indicates to the public that the person holding the certification has met the necessary minimum educational or experiential requirements for certification, has passed the certification examination, and has a responsibility to practice within certain rules, guidelines, or codes.

Licensure
Licensure, which is issued by the state and is usually the most rigorous form of monitoring, indicates to the public that the person holding the license has met the necessary minimum educational or experiential requirements for licensure, has passed the licensure examination, may perform certain specified tasks, such as counseling, psychotherapy, psychological assessment, and involuntary commitment of a dangerous client, and has the duty to practice within the rules or statutes as provided by law.

Processing Client Complaints and Sanctions

Professional organizations usually have an ethics codes and an ethics committee to oversee the practices of the members of the organization. Generally, when a complaint is filed with a professional organization against one of its members, the committee will evaluate the merit of the complaint. If found to have merit, further investigation is warranted and the practitioner is put on notice that a complaint has been filed against him or her. The practitioner will be given the opportunity to present his or her case within a specified period of time. Subsequent to the investigation, the committee meets and makes a determination whether the complaint will be dismissed in part or in total and whether any ethical standards have been violated, warranting sanctions. Possible sanctions by the professional organization are the issuance of a reprimand, monetary damages, member probation or suspension for a specified period of time, the issuance of a recommendation to the member to resign membership, the issuance of a recommendation that the member complete certain tasks such as personal therapy, further education, or ongoing supervision, and expulsion from the organization. The sanctions of suspension and expulsion typically are published in the organization's journal. It is important to note that professional organizations and certification boards may revoke membership or certification, however, without further discipline, the practitioner may still practice without the certification or membership.

Similar to the process of dealing with client complaints by professional organizations, licensing boards will usually have an appointed committee or council to review complaints, which will follow a statutorily proscribed course of investigation remarkably similar to that which is followed by professional organizations. The most significant difference is in terms of discipline. Because licensure is a creature of the state, as such, the investigation into complaints may result in more severe sanctions—for example, the prohibition of all practice on the practitioner's behalf in that state and criminal liability. In both arenas, the professional organization sanction and the licensure board sanction, the practitioner usually has some right to appeal. Another significant difference is that the standards set forth by licensing boards are often the minimum standards allowed for the field, whereas the ethical guidelines set forth by professional organizations are often aspirational.

Because client ethics complaints often precede civil lawsuits brought by the client or criminal lawsuits against the practitioner brought by the state, practitioners must remember that anything said in response to an inquiry from a professional organization or licensing board is admissible against the practitioner both in a civil malpractice trial and in a criminal trial. Practitioners should acquire malpractice insurance, which covers legal representation regarding client complaints to professional organizations and licensing boards. If there is a possibility that a malpractice case will be filed, it is highly recommended that the practitioner consult with a malpractice attorney before interaction with the professional association or licensing board.

Guidelines for Dealing with Client Complaints

- Practitioners must take all client complaints seriously and take all measures possible to protect the client where a dispute arises.
- When contacted by a professional organization or licensing board regarding a client complaint, practitioners should contact their malpractice carrier or an attorney for guidance as to how to respond.
- In all cases unless otherwise advised by legal counsel, when contacted by a professional organization or licensing board regarding a client complaint, the practitioner must respond within the time allotted by the professional organization or licensing board.
- Practitioners must ensure that the appropriate consent to release information is obtained from the client before providing any confidential information to a third party.
- Practitioners should remember that all information provided, statements made, and opinions garnered from the practitioner can and will be used against that practitioner if civil or criminal action is initiated against that practitioner.

COMPETENCY (CLIENT)

In certain circumstances, the law deems people as incompetent to make treatment or hospitalization decisions, to stand trial, to manage property, to enter into contracts, to marry, to execute a will, or to vote. Client incompetence is also sometimes used in decision making about child custody and placement. The question of whether a potential client can give consent or is incompetent to consent is an important professional and ethical challenge facing practitioners. Informed consent presupposes competence or the capacity to make an autonomous decision using a well-formed conscience and the ability to understand the nature of the agreement in order to make an informed consent for mental health treatment. Examples of clients who create the competency challenges for practitioners are those who are actively under the influence of a mind-altering substance, those who have neurological problems such as dementia, or those who are suffering from mental illness. In addition, client competency issues arise when practitioners use involuntary commitment or participate in forensic evaluations of client competency for other legal purposes.

Client Competence and Related Considerations

Client Competence

The definition of client competency seems to be a moving target and varies greatly depending on who is asked. The law draws distinctions between the types and degrees of mental incapacity depending on the particular issue involved. *Young v. State Dept. of Soc. Serv.*, 401 N.Y.S. 2d 955, 957 (1978), for example, stated a different showing is required to demonstrate incompetence with respect to contracts and gifts than is required with respect to competence to execute a will.

There is a broad and vague standard for incompetency in the context of informed consent to treatment and hospitalization. In the landmark case of *Zinermon v. Burch*, in the context of competency to consent to voluntary psychiatric hospitalization, the United States Supreme Court stated that the client had to be able to provide "express and informed consent," defined as "consent voluntarily given in writing after sufficient explanation and disclosure . . . to enable the person . . . to make a knowing and willful decision" and "to understand any proffered 'explanation and disclosure of the subject matter' of the [voluntary admission] forms that person is asked to sign" (*Zinermon v. Burch*, 494 U.S. at 133 [quoting FLA. STAT. §394.455 (22) 1981]).

A further example of the various standards of client competency is illustrated in *Dusky v. United States*, which is followed in substance by all jurisdictions (*Dusky v. United States*, 362 U.S. 402 [1960]). Therein, the United States Supreme Court stated that the standard for competency to stand trial is whether the defendant "has sufficient present ability to consult with his lawyer with a reasonable degree of rational understanding and whether he has a rational as well as factual understanding of the proceedings against him" (*Dusky v. United States*, 362 U.S. 402, 402 [1960]). Overall, it is imperative that the practitioner knows the state laws and regulations regarding client competency and the specific purpose for which the evaluation is being made, that is, consent for treatment, to stand trial. Accordingly, a potential client's competence to perform a specific task or role will not necessarily render the client legally incompetent to perform in other areas.

Involuntary Commitment
Most states have a procedure whereby a person who is at risk for harming himself or another can be involuntarily committed for a designated period of time during which a psychiatric evaluation will be conducted. At the expiration of the designated period of time, if the psychiatric evaluation recommends continued hospitalization and the client can not or will not voluntarily comply, a legal hearing must be held to determine whether to continue hospitalization.

Informed Consent to Treatment
The client's right to decide whether to participate in treatment after the practitioner fully describes the services to be rendered in a manner that is understandable by the client.

Legal and Ethical Aspects

Presumption of Competency
Most jurisdictions presently have a presumption in favor of competence in a majority of contexts. The U.S. Supreme Court in *Medina v. California* upheld the constitutionality of a state statute containing a presumption in favor of the competency of a criminal defendant to stand trial and placing the burden of proving incompetency by a preponderance of the evidence on the party raising the competency issues (*Medina v. California*, 505 U.S. 437 [1992]).

Mental Competency and Informed Consent to Treatment and Hospitalization
There is a broad standard for incompetency in the context of informed consent to treatment or hospitalization; however, in all jurisdictions, there is a mandate for mental health professionals to evaluate the competency of potential clients to consent to voluntary psychiatric hospitalization or treatment. In *Zinermon v. Burch*, voluntarily admitted patients alleged that they were heavily medicated, disoriented, and suffering from psychotic disorders when they were admitted to a Florida state mental health treatment facility and that consequently they were deprived of liberty without due process of law. Darrell E. Burch, the named patient in the case, alleged that the Florida state mental hospital violated the law by admitting him

185

voluntarily when the hospital "knew or should have known that [he] was incapable of voluntary, knowing, understanding and informed consent" to admission. The U.S. Supreme Court held that the hospital should have only allowed patients who were competent to consent to voluntary admission and that the defendants were liable as a result thereof. The Supreme Court's position in *Burch* is extremely important to all practitioners because a potential client may present as disoriented or distressed and as a result of the disturbance or confusion, there are indications that he or she is unable to provide informed consent, which, if ignored, opens the practitioner up to legal liability.

Additionally, concurrent with the client's execution of the voluntary admission document or informed consent, the practitioner must examine the client's documented behavior as recorded by other mental health professionals at the same facility. Interestingly, it was documented in Darrell Burch's nursing assessment almost immediately after his admission to the facility that he was confused, unable to state the reason for his hospitalization, and believed he was "in heaven." The psychiatrist in that case, Marlus Zinermon, wrote progress reports which reflected Burch's condition upon admission as disoriented, semimute, confused, and bizarre in appearance and thought, uncooperative at the initial interview, extremely psychotic, and apparently paranoid and hallucinating. Consultation with colleagues becomes increasingly important in the context of assessing a potential client's competency.

Mental Competency in Other Contexts
Practitioners and other mental health professionals are routinely engaged to perform forensic evaluations of a person's competency for legal purposes such as the person's competence to manage property, to enter into contracts, to marry, to execute a will, or to vote. It is important to note that competent written consent of the evaluee should still be obtained unless there is a court order requiring the evaluation and vitiating the consent requirement. In preparing forensic evaluations, the practitioner has the responsibility to evaluate client competency objectively and all findings should be capable of substantiation by information and techniques appropriate to the specific evaluation and context.

Finally, by definition, involuntary commitment removes the requirement of informed consent and, consequently, there is no requirement to establish competency before proceeding. The problem arises when the incompetent potential client is not likely to injure himself or others, nor is the self-neglect or refusal to care for himself threatening his well-being, and consequently does not meet the criteria for involuntary confinement and will likely not receive inpatient treatment.

Guidelines Regarding Client Mental Competency

- Practitioners must know their state laws and regulations regarding client competency and informed consent to treatment and involuntary commitment.
- Practitioners are advised to complete a full competency assessment, in the absence of involuntary commitment or a court order, before beginning counseling, performing a forensic evaluation, or admitting a client for voluntary admission into a treatment facility.
- If questions regarding a client's competency to voluntarily consent to treatment arise, practitioners should consult with a supervisor or consultant.

CONFIDENTIALITY, LIMITS TO

With every rule, there are exceptions. So, too, with the obligation of practitioners to protect the privacy of their clients from disclosure of their confidential communications. It is widely recognized that the duty to warn and the duty to protect create a "dangerous patient" exception to the practitioner's obligation of confidentiality. With some variations, the exception requires that practitioners warn individuals if a client's communications reflect a serious and imminent threat of harm to another and is likely the harm can be averted only by means of disclosure by the practitioner. In that same vein, most states require practitioners to breach their client's confidentiality when the client is in clear and imminent danger of suicide. Similarly, all states require practitioners to breach their client's confidentiality with some level of mandatory reporting, whereby practitioners are required to report known or suspected physical and sexual abuse and exploitation of certain vulnerable groups to the authorities.

The limits of confidentiality for minor clients are extensive. Practitioners are generally encouraged to maintain the confidentiality of minors in the same fashion as adults; however, legally, parents' rights to information about their children override the practitioner's ethical obligation of confidentiality. The legal rationale for allowing parents the right to confidentiality is based on the legal premise that minors are incompetent to give informed consent to treatment. In general, in addressing a minor client's suicide prevention and intervention, it is recommended that practitioners breach their minor client's confidentiality by informing the client's parents or guardians about the suicide risk for their children. Note that if the child's parents or guardians fail to act on prevention recommendations, the practitioner has an obligation to follow up with the minor child. There is a great deal of debate about whether the parents' legal right to know what occurs in their minor child's therapy is in the ultimate best interest of the child, but the law remains clear: parents have the right to know.

Overall, practitioners should note that a client's confidentiality is of paramount importance and breaching confidentiality should not be taken lightly. If the practitioner discovers that there is an exception to the obligation to protect the client's confidentiality, the practitioner needs to determine whether the law allows disclosure or requires it. Where the law allows it but does not require it, a particularly difficult situation is created for practitioners. The extent of the allowable or mandated disclosure and even the time frame will likely be specified in the law of the jurisdiction.

Limits to Confidentiality and Related Considerations

Confidentiality
The requirement, with some exceptions, that practitioners will not reveal to others the content of the information communicated by clients to them in therapy.

Practitioner-Client Privileged Communication
Practitioner-client privileged communication laws vary from state to state and the federal rule, but essentially all require, with some exceptions, that communications between a practitioner and a client are privileged and the practitioner cannot be forced to disclose such communications without the client's consent.

Duty to Warn
In general, the duty to warn creates an exception to the general rule of confidentiality and imposes a legal obligation on practitioners to contact and warn the intended victim when a client states in therapy an intent to harm a specific victim.

188

Duty to Protect

In general, the duty to protect goes beyond the duty to warn. Not only does it create an exception to the general rule of confidentiality and impose a legal obligation on practitioners to contact and warn the intended victim when a client states in therapy an intent to harm a specific victim, but it also requires the practitioner to take prompt, proactive measures to safeguard the intended victim (i.e., involving law enforcement).

Mandatory Reporting Laws

Mandatory reporting laws require practitioners to report known or suspected vulnerable groups from physical and sexual abuse and exploitation in a timely manner.

Physical Abuse

Physical abuse generally involves an act that results in nonaccidental physical injury or trauma (i.e., punching, beating, kicking, biting, burning, or otherwise harming another) and often the physical injury is a result of unreasonable, severe corporal punishment or unjustifiable punishment.

Sexual Abuse

Sexual abuse usually includes sexual assault (i.e., rape, incest, sodomy, or oral copulation) and sexual exploitation (e.g., employment of a minor to perform obscene acts or assisting a child to engage in prostitution).

Exploitation

Exploitation can be sexually or monetarily oriented, but it usually involves the act of taking unjust advantage of another for one's own benefit. An example of financial exploitation of the elderly would be a caretaker hired to care for an elderly person who requires the elderly person to purchase her various expensive gifts as a condition to continued care.

Neglect

Neglect generally refers to the maltreatment, indication of harm, or threats to a vulnerable person's health or welfare by any person. Neglect will usually include both overt acts (i.e., deliberate starving) and omissions (i.e., failure to get proper medical attention).

Guidelines for Addressing Limits to Confidentiality

- Practitioners need to know their state's mandatory reporting statute and learn which populations are considered vulnerable and the extent to which the practitioner may breach confidentiality.
- It is imperative for practitioners to know whether their state has a duty to warn and duty to protect statute and, if so, the extent to which the practitioner is obligated to exercise that duty.
- If a practitioner is going to treat children and adolescents, it is incumbent on the practitioner to familiarize himself or herself with the ethical and legal issues related to counseling children and adolescents.
- Practitioners should know and understand suicide risk factors, processes, and procedures for suicide risk assessment, and different tools for intervention.
- It is important for practitioners to stay current through professional development activities regarding ethical/legal issues in counseling.
- The "Consent for Treatment" form must clearly explain to the client the exceptions to confidentiality, including the duty to report suspected child abuse, elder abuse, or abuse of disabled persons to the state protection agency in your jurisdiction, the duty to warn and the duty to protect, the duty to keep parents of minors informed, and the duty to protect a client in the event of clear and imminent danger of suicide.
- When in doubt as to whether mandatory reporting requirements have been triggered, practitioners are urged to consider whether it would be helpful to seek supervision or consultation from trusted colleagues or legal counsel.
- When in doubt as to whether confidentiality can or must be breached, practitioners are encouraged to consider whether it would be helpful to seek supervision, consultation from trusted colleagues, or legal counsel.

CONFLICTS OF INTEREST

The relationship between a practitioner and client is unique. Therapy usually involves the unidirectional sharing of a client's innermost thoughts and feelings to the practitioner and not the reverse. The nature of the relationship revolves around helping the client and not the practitioner. There is an inherent imbalance in power because the practitioner is the holder of expert knowledge and the client generally defers to such knowledge. The ethical principle of beneficence requires that the practitioner act in the best interest of the client and develop treatment plans and interventions accordingly. The ethical principle of nonmalficence requires the practitioner to do no harm. Unfortunately, both ethical principles are jeopardized when conflicts of interest arises. Generally, a conflict of interest arises when a practitioner has competing interests that interfere with the practitioner's ability to faithfully exercise his or her professional judgment and skill in working with clients. For example, a conflict of interest arises where a practitioner sees his or her employer's child in therapy. The practitioner's desire to have her employer view her in a positive light is competing with effectively assessing and treating her employer's child and the practitioner's professional judgment may be impaired. Another example would be a supervisee who wishes to focus on psychoanalytic theory seeking supervision from a supervisor who has limited experience practicing using psychoanalytic theory. Instead of referring the supervisee to another supervisor who specializes in the psychoanalytic model, the supervisor agrees to supervise the supervisee in his use of the psychoanalytic model because business has been slow and he could use the money. The practitioner's judgment may be affected by the competing concern of increasing revenue for his business. In both examples, if the practitioner allows his or her own needs or interests (i.e., her desire to have her employer view her in a positive light and his desire to increase revenue) take precedence over the client's needs or interests, there is a conflict of interest which will likely do harm to the client. Dual or multiple relationships often create a conflict of interest because the practitioner has additional relationship factors to consider which may interfere with the practitioner's professional judgment. The practitioner must be mindful of the power differential and boundaries to avoid conflicts of interest and boundary violation.

Conflicts of Interest and Related Considerations

Conflict of Interest

A conflict of interest in counseling arises when a practitioner has competing interests that may interfere with the practitioner's duty to faithfully exercise his or her professional judgment and skill in working with a client. A conflict of interest in supervision can also arise when the supervisor has competing interests that may interfere with the supervisor's duty to exercise his or her professional judgment faithfully in working with the supervisee.

Boundary

A boundary can be defined as the frame and limits surrounding a therapeutic relationship that specifies a set of roles and rules for relating for both client and practitioner. Clients are in a vulnerable position because of the power differential between the practitioner and the client and boundaries serve to protect the client.

Boundary Crossing

A boundary crossing is a benign and typically beneficial departure from traditional expectations about the settings and constraint of clinical practice. Boundary crossings involve any deviation of clinical behavior from the standards of practice associated with traditional or conservative treatment approaches that emphasize emotional distance or reducing clinical risk and liability.

Boundary Violation

Boundary violations are exploitive or harmful practices in psychotherapy that occur when a practitioner violates standards of the profession for his or her own sexual, emotional, or financial gain.

Dual or Multiple Relationship

A dual relationship involves the practitioner playing both a professional role as the practitioner and an additional alternate role, such as landlord, employer, or friend. A multiple relationship involves the practitioner paying both the professional role as the practitioner and more than one additional alternate roles. Practitioners in dual or multiple relationships may have competing interests that interfere with the practitioner's duty to faithfully exercise his or her professional judgment and skill in working with a client and consequently a conflict of interest is created. It is important to note, however, that a dual or multiple relationship is not inherently wrong or conflicting, but there is always the risk of the practitioner abusing his or her power or losing objectivity.

Guidelines Regarding Conflicts of Interest

- Practitioners must review the code of ethics of your professional association and/or state or federal laws about a particular situation.

- In deciding what the best course of action to take may be in the particular situation, practitioners need to decide what ethical principle(s) guiding clinical behavior would be helpful.

- Practitioners should objectively assess the particular issue or circumstances from the perspective of the power differential between that practitioner and the client.

- In the practitioner's ethical decision making with regard to the client, such as financial concerns or emotional needs, the practitioner must evaluate what additional influences may be operative.

- In cases involving a potential conflict of interest, practitioners should always consider whether it would be helpful to seek supervision or consultation from trusted colleagues about this particular situation.

- It is absolutely essential for practitioners to practice self-care strategies to ensure their health.

DEPOSITIONS

Most practitioners are reluctant to get involved in litigation involving clients. With the recent increase in litigation, this will continue to become a reality for more practitioners. When served with a subpoena for deposition, practitioners will likely experience anxiety because they are being forced to enter an unfamiliar world with adversarial procedures. Practitioners may feel a sense of inadequacy within the legal system. When a subpoena orders a practitioner to appear at a deposition, the practitioner should consult an attorney and is required to respond in some fashion, whether by appearing at the deposition or motioning the court to quash the subpoena for a protective order. If employed, the practitioner should consult with a supervisor within the agency or facility and inquire as to whether the employer will provide legal counsel to represent the practitioner served with the deposition. If possible, practitioners should have an attorney present with them at the deposition because there will be no judge present to protect the practitioner whose deposition is being taken from the deposing attorneys. At a minimum, the attorney will familiarize the practitioner with the process and procedures of deposition taking and ideally will prepare the practitioner to answer the legal questions posed.

Depositions and Related Considerations

Subpoena

A legal document initiated by the judge or in some cases an attorney that requires the person being served with the subpoena to appear at a deposition or in court at a specified time, place, and date. In the absence of a court order excusing the person served with the subpoena, failure to appear as required could result in civil and criminal penalties for the person under subpoena.

Subpoena Duces Tecum

A legal document initiated by the judge—or, in some cases, an attorney—that requires the person being served with the subpoena to appear at a deposition or in court at a specified time, place, and date with a specific set of records that are requested directly on the subpoenas *duces tecum.*

Deposition

A method of discovery or gathering relevant information whereby attorneys either issue a subpoena or request that the court issue a subpoena, which requires a person to appear at a specified time, place (usually the attorney's office), and date for questioning of that person by the attorneys on both sides, all of which will be recorded by a court reporter. At the beginning of the deposition, the person whose deposition is being taken, often referred to as the deponent, will be sworn in by the court reporter and all testimony given will be under oath. Depositions generally serve one or both of two purposes, mainly to discover any evidence that could be used at trial and to preserve testimony. If the deponent is served with a subpoena *duces tecum,* which requires the deponent to produce document, the deponent is required to have a copy of the requested documents at the deposition.

Confidentiality

The requirement that practitioners will not reveal to others the content of the information communicated by clients to them in therapy.

Practitioner-Client Privileged Communication

Practitioner-client privileged communication laws vary from state to state and the federal rule, but essentially all require, with some exceptions, that communications between a practitioner and a client are privileged and the practitioner cannot be forced to disclose such communications without the client's consent.

Privilege and Depositions

A subpoena to appear for a deposition or to produce documents does not remove the practitioner's requirement and duty to keep the client's communications and records confidential. On receipt of a subpoena and after consultation with an attorney, a practitioner should contact the client and ask the client for his or her written consent to appear at the deposition. The client is the privilege holder and does not have to waive his or her right to confidentiality; however, often the client wants to waive his or her privilege, such as when the client is actually the plaintiff in a personal injury suit and request that the practitioner testify as to pain and suffering. If the client does not consent to waive the privilege, the practitioner may not say anything about the privileged communications nor may the practitioner release the client's confidential medical records unless an exception to the privilege exists or a court order requiring disclosure is obtained.

Practitioner Deposition Limitations

Attorneys are given a great deal of leeway with respect to the content of the questions posed to a practitioner and it is important for the practitioner to understand the limitations or lack thereof. First, as a practitioner, there is no right to personal privacy and, consequently, the deposing attorney can ask questions regarding your education, training, professional credentials, experience, and, unfortunately, your personal life. The deposing attorney may be seeking to attack the credibility of the deponent and may use the deposition as the forum for discrediting information. Second, in direct contravention to what can be asked of a witness in court, the attorney in a deposition can ask a practitioner to repeat hearsay, give opinions, or speculate. The practitioner must answer the question posed but may qualify his or her answer by stating that the question calls for speculation or an opinion. Third, the deposing attorney can generally continue the deposition from day to day during business hours, excluding holidays and weekends, in an effort to exhaust the deponent. Practitioners facing a deposition should familiarize themselves with state or local rules, which usually require breaks from questioning and may place restrictions on the length of the deposition and the ability of the deponent to consult with his or her counsel. Finally, the deposition is the attorneys' chance to observe and evaluate the practitioner as a witness before the actual trial and, as such, may attempt to fluster, anger, or "get a rise out of" the practitioner. Practitioners should remain at all times during the deposition calm, cool, and collected.

Guidelines for Practitioner's Depositions

- On receipt of a subpoena for deposition, a practitioner should contact and, if possible, retain an attorney to represent him or her and/ or appear at the deposition.

- If a practitioner receives a subpoena for deposition about a particular client, the practitioner should contact the client about whom the practitioner has been subpoenaed and ask that client for consent to appear at the deposition and/or release confidential information or records.

- If the client consents to waive his or her privilege, the practitioner should make all reasonable efforts to obtain the necessary written consent.

- Before participating in a deposition, practitioners should review the state and local rules regarding depositions, that is, length of time allowed, break requirements. Generally speaking, this information can be obtained at the local library.

- If an attorney advises a practitioner to attend the deposition, the practitioner needs to appear calm, cool, and collected during the entire deposition. The practitioner needs to make every effort to keep his or her anxiety level low and recognize that the attorney taking the deposition is purposely trying to "get a rise" out of the practitioner.

- If an attorney advises a practitioner to attend the deposition but the client has not consented to waive the practitioner-client privilege, the practitioner should only answer those questions that do not require the practitioner to reveal confidential communications from that practitioner's client.

- If an attorney advises a practitioner to attend the deposition and the client has consented to waive the practitioner-client privilege, the practitioner should answer all questions honestly, succinctly, and directly.

DIMINISHED CAPACITY

Diminished capacity, sometimes referred to as diminished responsibility, originated as a psychological term but is now frequently used as a legal term of art in criminal law. In some circumstances, practitioners will be in a position to evaluate whether a client has or had the mental capacity to perform or to have performed a certain act, task, or function. Most crimes require an *actus reus* or guilty act and a *mens rea* or mental element. In terms of criminal law, the legal concept of diminished capacity provides for a defendant to introduce evidence of mental abnormality as a defense, not amounting to insanity, to render him or her incapable of having the mental element required to commit the crime, exonerating the defendant of the charge. Diminished capacity is usually caused by intoxication, trauma, depression, frontal lobe dysfunction, or mental disease; however, this list is not intended to be exhaustive or exclusive. Perhaps the most notorious case in which a diminished capacity defense was successfully employed was in *People v. Dan White*, which became popularly referred to as the case in which the defendant successfully asserted the "Twinkie Defense." Therein, the admitted killer of San Francisco Mayor George Moscone and Supervisor Harvey Milk was convicted only of manslaughter as apposed to first-degree murder based on his allegation that as a result of his diminished capacity, mainly depression, he was not capable of the premeditation required to support a charge of first-degree murder.

The legal concept of diminished capacity also has been used to reduce the degree of crime for which the defendant may be convicted, even if the defendant's conduct satisfied all the formal elements of a higher offense. For example, a penal code may define second-degree murder as causing the death of a person, which is the guilty act, with the intent to cause the death of a person, which is the mental element. By contrast, second-degree manslaughter may be defined as causing the death of a person, which is the guilty act, recklessly, which is the mental element. In this example, second-degree manslaughter is clearly the lesser offense. A defendant who successfully asserts a diminished capacity defense in this case would be convicted on second-degree manslaughter notwithstanding having met the elements of second-degree murder. Overall, the successful use of the diminished capacity defense in those jurisdictions that recognize it often will lead to conviction of a lesser crime, with mitigated punishment.

197

In terms of civil law, practitioners also may be engaged to perform forensic evaluations of a person's capacity or competency for other legal purposes such as the person's ability to modify a will, enter into contract, or care for a child. Outside the criminal law arena, diminished capacity may be used synonymously with mental incompetence or as a lesser degree of mental incompetence.

Diminished Capacity and Related Considerations

Capacity

Capacity is the mental ability to know and understand the nature and potential consequences of one's own actions.

Diminished Capacity

In general terms, diminished capacity describes one who does not have the mental ability to know or understand the nature and potential consequence of one's own actions. When used as a legal definition in criminal law, diminished capacity is a defense to a criminal charge wherein a defendant alleges that he or she had diminished capacity or an impaired mental condition at the time of the alleged offense such that he or she was unable to have the requisite mental state to be convicted of the crime or that the penalty for such crime is reduced.

Informed Consent to Treatment

The client's right to decide whether to participate in treatment after the practitioner fully describes the services to be rendered in a manner that is understandable by the client.

Diminished Capacity and Consent for Treatment

Often, practitioners work with clients who are not able to give consent as a result of diminished capacity or mental incompetency. The practitioner's utmost concern needs to be to protect the rights of those clients who do not possess the capacity or who suffer from diminished capacity to make free choices regarding their participation in counseling.

Guidelines for Addressing Diminished Capacity

- Practitioners must know their state law regarding diminished capacity and whether that practitioner's jurisdiction recognizes the defense of diminished capacity.
- Practitioners need to acknowledge and accept their level of competence, experience, and training and make every effort not to exceed it; if a practitioner does not feel as though he or she is competent to offer an opinion on an issue, it is best not to.
- It is imperative for practitioners to understand the nature of the task for which he or she has been assigned and realize that different tasks have different standards (i.e., criminal law versus civil law).
- In the absence of involuntary commitment or a court order, before beginning counseling, performing a forensic evaluation, or admitting a client for voluntary admission into a treatment facility, the practitioner is advised to complete a full competency assessment.
- The practitioner should familiarize himself or herself with the elements of each crime about which the practitioner will evaluate a defendant for diminished capacity, as this is a potentially complicated matter, particularly with regard to whether the offense requires that the defendant have the intent to accomplish the specific act charged.
- If retained as an expert witness, the practitioner should testify in an objective and candid manner, regardless of which party retained that practitioner.
- When applicable, practitioners are advised to educate the attorney about the issues of diminished capacity as the attorney may be unaware of the issues.
- If questions regarding a client's capacity arise, practitioners are urged to consult with a supervisor or consultant.

DUTIES TO THIRD PARTIES

The concept of duty is legally created. It is clear that practitioners have an ethical and a legal (contract) duty of care to their clients. Practitioners also have a duty to certain third parties. In the realm of practitioner duties to third parties created by contract, as an employee of a clinic, the practitioner has a duty not only to the client but also to the clinic, the supervisor, and the clinic administration. The practitioner also may have a duty to a third-party payor, such as a managed care company. As a result of the consequent duties created by a written or oral contract, in the clinical context, the practitioner has an obligation to the other party to the contract or contracts as well as to the client.

It becomes less clear when considering whether practitioners have ethical and legal duties to third parties who are not party to a written or oral contract. Sometimes the practitioner may have a duty to a third party whom he or she has never even met or with whom the practitioner has no contractual ties. In essence, without a contractual relationship between the practitioner or supervisor and the third party, in order to recover in a tort action against a practitioner or a supervisor, the plaintiff/third party has to prove that the practitioner had a duty to the plaintiff/ third party. For example, most states and professional organizations have created a practitioner duty to warn and duty to protect an intended victim when a client states an intent to harm that specific victim. Consequently, the third party or intended victim may proceed against the practitioner even though there was no contract between the intended victim and the practitioner. Taking it even one step further, the supervisor of the practitioner has a duty to the client, with whom the supervisor may never work directly, and the intended victim. As a result of these duties, the client and the intended victim may bring a tort action against the supervisor. In some cases, courts have determined that a practitioner owes a duty to family members of a client and, accordingly, those family members may be able to sue a practitioner for their own harm, even if the client declines or is unable to sue. An example arises in cases in which a practitioner is treating a child. The practitioner has a clear duty not only to the child who is being treated but also to the parents of the child in that the parents have a right to know about the child's clinical treatment. Consequently, in most jurisdictions, parents have the right to proceed against practitioners on behalf of their children.

States vary widely with regard to which third parties a practitioner owes a legal duty; however, the allegation that there existed a duty is always a necessary element in a malpractice action. Practitioners need to be particularly concerned when their duties to various parties conflict with one another.

Duties to Third Parties and Related Considerations

Duty
An obligation arising out of a contract or operation of law, which requires a practitioner to take or refrain from action, perform in a certain fashion, or maintain a standard of care. A breach of a duty under contract or operation of law may subject the practitioner to civil liability under contract or tort law.

Liability
Generally, a legal obligation, monetary or otherwise, that a practitioner or supervisor has incurred or may incur as a result of a negligent act and/or malpractice of the practitioner, supervisee, or supervisor.

Tort
A tort is an act or wrongdoing not arising out of a contract that causes injury to a potential plaintiff in some fashion, and for which the potential plaintiff may sue the tortfeasor or person whose act or wrongdoing caused the injury for civil damages. Actions for negligence and malpractice are tort actions.

Malpractice
In the clinical context, malpractice is a form of negligence that requires four specific elements to be met. Essentially, in order to prove a case of negligence, the plaintiff must show that at the time of the alleged negligent incident, a legal duty between the practitioner and the client existed, the practitioner breached that duty, and that the client suffered harm or injury that was directly and proximately caused by the practitioner's breach of duty.

Guidelines for Duties to Third Parties

- Practitioners are advised to acknowledge all parties to whom that practitioner owes a duty based on contract, recognizing that a contract with a third party may be oral as well as written.
- Practitioners should be cognizant of all third parties to whom that practitioner's state acknowledges a practitioner owes a duty and if practicable, learn the extent to which the duty obligates each individual practitioner.
- As a way of reducing the risk of a breach of duty to either a client or a third party or parties, practitioners are encouraged to practice self

201

care strategies regularly and consistently, especially during times of stress in their own personal life.

- Practitioners should consider whether it would be helpful to seek supervision or consultation from trusted colleagues about a particular situation that involves a conflict between the duty owed to a client and the duty owed to a third party.
- Practitioners must recognize and understand that they may be held liable under tort or contract law for a breach of duty and govern their actions accordingly.

DUTY TO WARN AND DUTY TO PROTECT

The *Tarasoff v. Regents of the University of California*, 551 P.2d 334, 345 (Cal. 1976) decision by the Supreme Court of California set the stage for a series of groundbreaking cases that held that once a psychotherapist determines or reasonably should have determined that a client poses a serious danger of violence to others, the psychotherapist bears a duty to exercise reasonable care to protect the foreseeable victim of that danger, notwithstanding confidentiality and the general rule at common law that one person owes neither a duty to control the conduct of another nor a duty to warn those endangered by such conduct. In the *Tarasoff* case, Prosenjit Poddar, a client in therapy, made a threat against Tatiana Tarasoff, a woman who had rebuffed him romantically, to his psychotherapist. The psychotherapist attempted unsuccessfully to have Mr. Poddar involuntarily committed and Mr. Poddar discontinued therapy. Two months after Mr. Poddar's disclosure to his psychotherapist of his threat to harm Ms. Tarasoff, Mr. Poddar actually murdered Ms. Tarasoff. The Tarasoff Court assessed liability for the failure of the psychotherapist to warn Ms. Tarasoff of the danger to her. Court rulings following the *Tarasoff* decision have adopted, clarified, and, to some extent, limited the violation of client confidentiality only when the client states an intent to harm a specific intended victim. Currently, most states and professional organizations have created a duty to warn and duty to protect. Generally, when a client states an intent to harm a specific victim, practitioners must attempt to contact both the intended victim and local law enforcement to fully comply with the duty to warn and duty to protect.

Duty to Warn and Protect and Related Considerations

Confidentiality

The requirement, with some exceptions, that practitioners will not reveal to others the content of the information communicated by clients to them in therapy.

Practitioner-Client Privileged Communication

Practitioner-client privileged communication laws vary from state to state and the federal rule, but essentially all require, with some exceptions, that communications between a practitioner and a client are privileged and the practitioner cannot be forced to disclose such communications without the client's consent.

Duty to Warn

In general, the duty to warn creates an exception to the general rule of confidentiality and imposes a legal obligation on practitioners to contact and warn the intended victim when a client states in therapy an intent to harm a specific victim.

Duty to Protect

In general, the duty to protect goes beyond the duty to warn. Not only does it create an exception to the general rule of confidentiality and impose a legal obligation on practitioners to contact and warn the intended victim when a client states in therapy an intent to harm a specific victim, but it also requires the practitioner to take prompt, proactive measures to safeguard the intended victim (i.e., involving law enforcement).

Duty to Warn and Protect with HIV-Positive Clients

The increase in the spread of AIDS presents a particular challenge for practitioners in determining whether there is a duty to warn identifiable or readily identifiable sexual or needle-sharing partners of those HIV-positive clients who may be at risk for acquiring the infection. State laws regarding the duty to warn and protect with HIV-positive clients vary considerably and some states even prohibit practitioners from warning identifiable victims of persons who are HIV-positive. For example, the court in *Reisner v. Regents of Univ. of Cal.*, 37 Cal Rptr. 2d 518 (1995) held a physician who failed to notify a client of her HIV status liable to her sexual partner who also contracted the infection from her. This holding seems to suggest that there is a duty to warn with regarding to HIV-positive clients; however, it is in direct contravention to the court's holding in *N.O.L. v. District of Columbia,* 674 A.2d 498 (D.C. 1995). The N.O.L. court decided that not only is there no duty on the part of health care providers to warn a husband of his wife's HIV status, but that the law actually prohibits disclosure of the HIV status of a client to his or her spouse.

Threats of Violence from a Nonclient Source

The duty to warn and protect also may extend to those communications regarding a client's threats received from someone other than the client. The court in *Ewing v. Goldstein,* (2004) 120 Cal.App.4th 807 [15 Cal.Rptr.3d 864] examined this specific issue. In *Ewing,* the practitioner treated the client for work-related emotional problems and problems concerning his former girlfriend. During the course of therapy, the client told his father that he was considering causing harm to his former's girlfriend's new boyfriend and the father contacted the practitioner and told him what the client had said. The client subsequently murdered the boyfriend and then committed suicide. The parents sued the practitioner for wrongful death based on the practitioner's failure to warn the victim after the practitioner received a communication that the client threatened to kill or cause serious physical harm to the victim. The *Ewing* court held that a communication from a family member to a practitioner, made for the purpose of advancing a client's therapy, was a "patient communication" within the meaning of the duty to warn law and as such, there was a duty to inform the intended victim of the threat. Whether the holding in the *Ewing* case will be adopted by other states remains to be seen.

Practitioner Immunity from Suit

When a practitioner warns a third party of a threat of harm without the client's consent, the practitioner may be sued and may even be found liable for the breach of confidentiality or defamation. The law in many states provides for absolute immunity from civil action for a practitioner who discloses a confidence to third parties in an effort to discharge a "duty to warn" of a client who makes threats of violence. Many other states, however, simply impose the duty to report, without providing a concomitant immunity from civil liability for the reporter. Where there is no statutory or case law provision for absolute privilege, courts generally extend a conditional or qualified privilege to report defamatory information where the reporter has a legal duty to do so.

Guidelines for Adhering to the Duty to Warn and the Duty to Protect

- Practitioners must know whether their state has a duty to warn and duty to protect statute and, if so, learn the extent to which practitioners are obligated to exercise their duty.
- Practitioners are advised to take proactive measures by planning potential action strategies that could be implemented in the event of a client threatening to harm a third party.
- Practitioners should assess the dangerousness of the client on an ongoing process, not a one-time event.
- Each and every threat to harm made by a client must be taken seriously by practitioners.
- When in doubt as to whether the duty to warn has been triggered, practitioners are encouraged to consider whether it would be helpful to seek supervision, consultation from a trusted colleagues, or legal counsel.

END-OF-LIFE CONSIDERATIONS

A practitioner's role in working with a client at the end of life can be dramatically different from that taken when working with clients at any other stage of life. As a client approaches the end of his or her life, he or she is facing a great deal of decisions that may have serious psychosocial implications for the client, and his or her friends, family, and loved ones. Dying clients are forced to deal with certain loss indicators during the course of the dying process, such as needing a feeding tube when one can no longer feed himself or herself or deciding when and if hospice care is appropriate.

Practitioners also need to recognize the legal and ethical implications that arise in working with clients with end-of-life issues. The Oregon Death with Dignity Act of 1997 legalizes physician-assisted suicide in Oregon and more states may follow suit. Practitioners working with clients with end-of-life issues need to be prepared to deal with clients who are facing their own mortality and struggling with the decision of whether to hasten their own death or employ another to assist in their suicide. Practitioner working with dying clients also must be prepared to educate clients regarding the necessary paperwork associated with the end of life, such as to assign a health care proxy or provide advanced directives.

Finally, practitioners may find themselves in varying roles throughout the process for the dying client. Some examples may be that of an advocate for assuring the client's quality of care, a facilitator for understanding multiple legal documents which are important at the end of life, an educator focused on improving the client and the client's family's knowledge about the process of dying and death, and a liaison between the dying individual and the medical team. Additionally, the practitioner may find himself or herself performing tasks that would normally not be performed for a nondying client. For example, the practitioner may write a letter to a client's loved one as dictated by the client or may assist the client in taking necessary medications. Another aspect that varies for the practitioner working with clients who are dying is that clinical work may take place in nontraditional settings, such as the client's home or the hospital. Professional boundaries may be more flexible than those a practitioner must have when working with other populations. Finally, the practitioner's focus might be more on daily decision making and emotional support.

End-of-Life Clients and Related Considerations

Hospice
At any time during a terminal illness, a client may consider hospice care. Although programs may vary by region, in general, hospice provides a comprehensive program of care to clients with a life-threatening illness and their families. Hospice programs emphasize palliative rather than curative treatment and frequently will provide the client care in their own home. Hospice neither hastens nor prolongs death.

Advance Care Directives
Advanced care directives are specific instructions, prepared in advance of death or incapacitation, which are intended to direct a person's medical care if he or she becomes unable to do so in the future. For example, someone may wish to refuse being fed through a tube or may wish not to be resuscitated once dead.

Health Care Proxy
A legal document that allows someone to appoint someone else as his or her proxy, to stand in his or her shoes and make medical or health care decisions, in the event the individual becomes unable to make and/or communicate such decisions himself or herself.

Assisted Suicide
Commonly involves the voluntary provision of assistance in the suicide of someone with a terminal illness who chooses to end his or her life.

Oregon Death with Dignity Act of 1997
In *Vacco v. Quill* and *Washington v. Glucksberg,* the United States Supreme Court ruled that assisted suicide is not a constitutionally protected right and that the legality of physician-assisted suicide should be decided by the states. The Oregon Death with Dignity Act of 1997 is Oregon state legislation that allows legal physician-assisted suicide under certain prescribed circumstances. The Act requires a physician to get a mental health evaluation when he or she believes that the patient may be suffering from a psychiatric disorder or depression that causes impaired judgment before the physician may assist the patient with suicide.

Hastened Death
Although there is a great deal of discussion in the literature about the definition of hastened death, generally this refers to someone with a terminal illness voluntarily stopping eating and drinking, terminating life support when dependent on it, or stopping aggressive treatment designated to stop the progression of an illness.

Do Not Resuscitate Request
A do not resuscitate request from a patient informs medical professionals that the patient has asked that no attempt be made to revive him or her once dead.

American Psychological Association on Assisted Suicide

In 1997, the American Psychological Public Communications Office and Public Interest Directorate published a briefing paper on the mental health issues involved in physician-assisted suicide and other end-of-life decisions intended to inform news media coverage about assisted suicide. In February 2001, the American Psychological Association released the American Psychological Resolution Council Resolution on

Assisted Suicide. Therein, it was resolved that the American Psychological Association took a position that neither endorses nor opposes assisted suicide.

National Association of Social Workers on Assisted Suicide

The National Association of Social Workers has taken a strong interest working toward policy change to improve the care of clients living with life-limiting illness and the dying. The Association states that "when confronting ethical dilemmas in palliative and end of life care, social workers can draw on the principle of client self-determination in matters where clients or their proxies are faced with such issues." Although the National Association of Social Workers does not take a position concerning the morality of end-of-life decisions, it specifically endorses the view that "social workers should be free to participate or not in assisted-suicide matters or other discussions concerning end-of-life decisions depending on their own beliefs, attitudes, and value systems." It is stressed that if a social worker has a problem helping with decisions about assisted suicide or other end-of-life choices, there is a professional obligation to make a referral to another professional who is competent to deal with the subject issues. The National Association of Social Workers does state, however, social workers in their professional capacity should not deliver, supply, or personally participate in an act of assisted suicide.

Guidelines for Working with Clients with End of Life Issues

- Practitioners should familiarize themselves with the available literature about death and dying issues.
- It is important for practitioners to know the ethics codes and criminal and civil legal statutes in their state or jurisdiction regarding advanced directives, health care proxy, hastened death, assisted suicide, and physician-assisted suicide.
- Practitioners should examine their own personal moral and ethical beliefs on hastened death, assisted suicide, and physician-assisted suicide.
- Practitioners are advised to offer support, understanding, and compassion to their clients regardless of whether the practitioner agrees with his or her end-of-life decisions.

- Practitioners must recognize the strong influence they may have with clients considering assisted suicide.
- In addressing the dying client's family, the practitioner must understand his or her role.
- It is incumbent on practitioners working closely with death and dying issues to employ a strong support system to handle issues of loss, grief, vulnerability, and traumatization that are common with that population.
- Practitioners should consider whether it would be helpful to seek supervision or consultation from a trusted colleague about any particular situation involving a dying client with which the practitioner is uncomfortable.

EXPERT TESTIMONY I: GENERAL CONSIDERATIONS

For many practitioners, the thought of testifying in a deposition or in court provokes extreme anxiety. A practitioner may serve as a fact witness with regard to a client (and testify only as to facts) or an expert witness. An expert witness is generally retained by either or both of the parties or is appointed by the court to evaluate some facet of a legal case. Generally, what differentiates the expert witness from a fact witness is that the expert is allowed to testify as to his or her opinion on an aspect of a case. For example, a practitioner might be retained by one party to a child custody dispute to testify regarding his or her expert opinion with regard to how it is in the child's best interest to reside with that party rather than the other. This expert opinion can be communicated by written report, deposition, or courtroom testimony. The testifying expert witness has to be qualified by the judge before opinion testimony will be admitted and the court will generally look to the *Frye* test or some other means through which the court can evaluate whether the expert testimony should be admitted and whether the witness has the requisite clinical experience and academic achievement to form an objective expert opinion to a reasonable degree of certainty. In any legal proceeding, an expert witness is obligated to testify in an objective and candid manner, regardless of which party retained that expert. Practitioners should remain at all times during the deposition or courtroom testimony calm, cool, and collected.

Expert Testimony and Related Considerations

Expert
A person who, by virtue of training or experience, has developed specialized knowledge on a particular subject so that he or she is able to form an opinion that a person without such knowledge could not provide.

Testifying Expert
An expert who is identified by a party in litigation as a potential expert witness for trial.

Subpoena
A legal document initiated by the judge—or, in some cases, an attorney—that requires the person being served with the subpoena to appear at a deposition or in court at a specified time, place, and date, and, if it is a subpoena *duces tecum,* with records requested by the subpoenas *duces tecum.*

Deposition
A deposition is a method of discovery or gathering relevant information whereby attorneys either issue a subpoena or request that the court issue a subpoena, which requires a deponent to appear at a specified time, place (usually the attorney's office), and date for questioning by the attorneys on both sides of the deponent under oath, all of which will be recorded by a court reporter. Depositions generally serve one or both of two purposes, mainly to discover any evidence that could be used at trial and to preserve testimony. If the deponent is served with a subpoena *duces tecum,* which requires the deponent to produce document, the deponent is required to have a copy of the requested documents at the deposition.

Confidentiality
The requirement that practitioners will not reveal to others the content of the information communicated by clients to them in therapy.

Practitioner-Client Privileged Communication
Practitioner-client privileged communication laws vary from state to state and the federal rule, but essentially all require, with some exceptions, that communications between a practitioner and a client are privileged and the practitioner cannot be forced to disclose such communications without the client's consent.

The *Frye* Test

The U.S. Court of Appeals for District of Colombia decided that a party seeking to introduce expert opinion testimony as to a certain topic must demonstrate that the basis on which the opinion is formed is sufficiently established to have gained general acceptance in the particular field to which it belongs (*Frye v. United States*, 293 F.1013 [D.C. Cir. 1923]).

Privilege and Expert Testimony

Qualification as an expert does not vitiate the practitioner's requirement to keep the client's communications confidential. A practitioner should contact the client and ask the client for his or her written consent before being testifying as an expert witness. The client is the privilege holder and does not have to waive his or her right to confidentiality; however, often the client wants to waive his or her privilege. If the client does not consent to waive the privilege, the practitioner may not say anything about the privileged communications unless an exception to the privilege exists or a court order requiring disclosure is obtained.

Testimony Limitations

Attorneys are given a great deal of leeway with respect to the content of the questions posed to an expert witness and it is important for the practitioner to understand the limitations or lack thereof. First, as a practitioner, there is no right to personal privacy and, consequently, the attorneys can ask questions regarding your education, training, professional credentials, experience, and, unfortunately, your personal life. The attorney may be seeking to attack the credibility of the expert witness and may use the deposition or the courtroom as the forum for discovering or introducing discrediting information. Second, the practitioner must answer any question posed (unless an objection is sustained by the court) but may qualify his or her answer by stating that the question calls for speculation or an opinion.

211

Guidelines for Expert Testimony

- Practitioners should testify in an objective and candid manner, regardless of which party retained the practitioner.
- It is important for the practitioner to remain at all times during a deposition or courtroom testimony calm, cool, and collected.
- Practitioners must tell the truth always.
- Practitioners should be prepared to testify by thoroughly reviewing his or her records and any prior testimony that practitioner may have given about the case and, if possible, rehearse his or her responses with the attorney who retained the practitioner.
- Practitioners are advised not bring to a deposition or court any documents that are not specifically requested.
- When testifying, the practitioner should answer only the question posed by the attorney and only answer if the practitioner knows the answer.
- A practitioner should remember that the attorney representing the party against whom that practitioner may be offering unfavorable testimony is going to make every effort to discredit that practitioner's testimony.
- It is essential for practitioners to know their level of competence, experience, and training, and not to exceed it. When a practitioner does not feel as though he or she is competent to offer an opinion on an issue, it is best not to.
- If a practitioner has previously testified, even if in another case, the practitioner should obtain a copy of the transcripts and review them carefully before testifying again.
- If necessary, educate the attorney regarding your area of expertise and field.

EXPERT TESTIMONY II: *FRYE* AND *DAUBERT*

Many cases involve the use of an expert witness or several expert witnesses who among other things introduce scientific testimony into the court proceedings. An expert witness is generally retained by either or both of the parties or is appointed by the court to evaluate some facet of a legal case. Generally, what differentiates the expert witness from a fact witness is that the expert is allowed to testify as to his or her opinion on an aspect of a case. Since the early 1900s, courts have attempted to limit the uncertainty of expert testimony presented in both criminal and civil trials by creating an evidentiary standard of reliability for scientific proof.

Expert Scientific Testimony Terms and Related Considerations

Expert
A person who, by virtue of training or experience, has developed specialized knowledge on a particular subject so that he or she is able to form an opinion that a person without such knowledge could not provide.

Testifying Expert
An expert who is identified by a party in litigation as a potential expert witness for trial.

The *Frye* Test
A party seeking to introduce expert opinion testimony as to a certain topic must demonstrate that the basis on which the opinion is formed is sufficiently established to have gained general acceptance in the particular field to which it belongs (*Frye v. United States*, 293 F.1013 [D.C. Cir. 1923]).

The *Daubert* Standard
A party seeking.to introduce expert opinion testimony as to a certain topic must demonstrate that the basis on which the opinion is formed is both reliable and relevant. The trial judge is the gatekeeper who shall determine the reliability and relevancy of the basis. The *Daubert* Standard includes several factors to which the court may look in determining whether the expert testimony is reliable.

Tests for Introducing Scientific and Technical Testimony

In *Frye v. United States*, 293 F.1013 (D.C. Cir. 1923), the U.S. Court of Appeals for the District of Columbia decided that a party seeking to introduce expert knowledge must demonstrate its "general acceptance." In this case, the defendant attempted to introduce expert evidence concerning a systolic blood pressure deception test, a precursor to the modern polygraph test, but the court excluded the evidence. The court stated, "While courts will go a long way in admitting expert testimony deduced from a well-recognized scientific principle or discovery, the thing from which the deduction is made must be sufficiently established to have gained general acceptance in the particular field to which it belongs." The *Frye* rule was followed by most courts until 1975 when the Federal Rules of Evidence were enacted. The majority of courts continued to apply the *Frye* test; however, the new standard of "factual assistance" created under the Federal Rules conflicted with the *Frye* test. In 1999, the U.S. Supreme Court resolved the conflict in the *Daubert v. Merrell Dow Pharmaceuticals, Inc.*, 509 U.S. 579 (1993). In *Daubert*, the Court ruled that the Federal Rules of Evidence regarding the admission of expert testimony supersede the *Frye* test. The case involved a claim against Merrell Dow Pharmaceuticals where the plaintiff's experts based their testimony on animal studies because there was no research done on humans. The *Daubert* court held that the trial judge is the "gatekeeper" of the relevancy and reliability of expert testimony. The *Daubert* Standard set forth specific factors that might "bear on" a judge's gatekeeping determination of whether the expert testimony is reliable:

1. Whether a "theory or technique . . . can be (and has been) tested";
2. Whether it "has been subjected to a peer review and publication";
3. Whether, in respect to a particular technique, there is a high "known or potential rate of error" and whether there are "standards controlling the technique's operation"; and
4. Whether the theory or technique enjoys "general acceptance" within a "relevant scientific community."

Finally, the U.S. Supreme Court, refusing to make a distinction between scientific knowledge and technical or other specialized knowledge, stated that the *Daubert* holding applies to all expert witnesses (*Kumho Tire Co., Ltd. v. Carmichael*, 526 U.S. 137 [1999]).

Guidelines for Admissibility of Scientific and Technical Expert Testimony

- Practitioners must know their state's law regarding the admissibility of scientific testimony. Generally speaking, this information can be obtained at the local library.
- Practitioners are advised to stay within their level of competence, experience, and training. If a practitioners does not feel as though he or she is competent to offer an opinion on an issue, it is best not to.
- Before testifying, practitioners must prepare themselves to respond to each of the four reliability prongs enunciated in the *Daubert* Standard.
- If necessary, educate the attorney regarding your area of expertise and field.

- If a practitioner has previously testified, even if in another case, the practitioner should obtain copies of the transcripts and review them carefully before testifying. The practitioner should be prepared to inform the fact finder regarding the details of past expert testimony experience.

HEALTH INSURANCE PORTABILITY AND ACCOUNTABILITY ACT (HIPAA)

The Health Insurance Portability and Accountability Act of 1996 (HIPAA) is federal legislation that requires organizations that provide or manage medical or psychotherapy services to be responsible and accountable for the policies and procedures used to protect client's confidential health information. It was created in an effort to provide a uniform and consistent set of procedures across the United States for the protection of health information in light of the increase in electronic database storage and instantaneous transmission of data. HIPAA has a Privacy Rule and a Security Rule. Specifically, the Privacy Rule of HIPAA indicates how information is disseminated to clients and made available to others and gives clients control over when and how their protected health information is disclosed for any purposes. Perhaps most important, the Privacy Rule, with certain exceptions, requires practitioners to take all reasonable steps to limit the use or disclosure of protected health information to the minimum necessary to accomplish the intended purpose. Although there are certain exceptions, the Privacy Rule also requires practitioners to act as though a client's legal personal representative was actually the client with regard to consent for treatment and access to medical records. Under HIPAA, the client or the client's personal representative has the right to authorize and then revoke an authorization to disclose the client's confidential information. The Security Rule of HIPAA provides the requirements for practitioners in the safeguarding, including physical, administrative, and technical safeguarding, preserving, and maintaining of client files by creating and adhering to written policies and procedures.

HIPAA and Related Considerations

Protected Health Information

HIPAA defines protected health information as information whether oral or recorded in any form that is created by a health care provider and relates to the past, present, or future physical or mental health or condition of an individual, the provision of health care to an individual, or the past present or future payment for the provision of health care to an individual that is transmitted or maintained by electronic media (including but not limited to the Internet, dial up phone lines, private networks, compact discs, or floppy disks) or any other form or medium. In essence, even though there is no case law deciphering HIPAA at this point, it appears that all information about a client would be considered protected health information.

Confidentiality
The requirement of practitioners to respect the privacy of clients by not providing to third parties the information communicated to them by clients during counseling sessions or the practitioner's impressions, diagnosis, assessment, or treatment plan of or for the client.

Privacy
Privacy is a right of the client to control his or her protected health care information and to prevent the unauthorized disclosure of such information.

Security
Security is the tools and safeguards through which the client's confidentiality is protected by the practitioner.

Administrative Safeguards
HIPAA has nine standards that address administrative safeguards, each of which limit access to protected health information to those authorized and to prevent those who are unauthorized, whether workforce members or others, from obtaining access to electronic protected health information. For example, an employer might only allow practitioners rather than all employees access to the computer files that contain diagnostic information or progress notes.

Physical Safeguards
HIPAA has four standards that address physical safeguards, each of which require the protection of the integrity and security of the physical locations where protected health information is stored and accessed. For example, a facility is required to create and maintain retrievable exact copies of all electronic protected health information in case of an emergency.

Technical Safeguards

HIPAA has five standards that address technical safeguards, each of which require the creation and implementation of policies and procedures to protect from unauthorized access, alteration, or destruction of electronic protected health information. For example, a facility may employ software that can protect against viruses or corruption to protect client information.

Exceptions to the Minimum Necessary Standard

The Minimum Necessary Standard applies in all disclosures except disclosures to or requests by a health care provider for treatment purposes, disclosures to the client or the client's personal representative, uses or disclosures made as authorized by the client or required under HIPAA, or uses or disclosures that are required by other laws.

Conflict of Laws

Most states have laws requiring protection of some forms of protected health information. HIPAA creates the minimum standard by which health care professionals must protect their client's protected health care information and does not replace already existing state or federal laws that grant individuals more privacy protections than HIPAA. Where there is conflict between the state or another federal law and HIPAA, the practitioner must follow that which grants the greatest protection to the client's privacy.

Penalties for Failure to Comply

The Department of Health and Human Services is authorized to take administrative action, civil penalties of no more than $100 for each violation, with the total amount imposed on a single practitioner for all violations of an identical requirement or prohibition during a calendar year not to exceed $25,000, and, in the case of fully disclosing a client's identifiable health information, fines up to $250,000 and imprisonment for up to 10 years.

Guidelines Regarding HIPAA

- Practitioners must know the HIPAA requirements and the specific state requirements regarding client privacy and security in their jurisdiction.

- Practitioners are advised to implement the HIPAA Privacy and Security rules in practice so long as their state or jurisdiction does not require a higher level of protection of private client information.
- Practitioners should take all reasonable steps to limit the use or disclosure of protected health information to the minimum necessary to accomplish the intended purpose.
- Practitioners are encouraged to consider whether it would be helpful to seek legal advice in the creation and implementation of HIPAA policies and procedures.

LIABILITY IN SUPERVISION: DIRECT AND INDIRECT

Supervision plays a critical role in practitioner development and most states require practitioners to undergo a period of supervision before practicing professionally. Most practitioners are aware of the legal risks of direct service provision; however, there seems to be less awareness about those cases in which a supervisor may be held vicariously or directly liable for the acts of a supervisee. The supervisor has the dual responsibilities of insuring that the supervisee performs in the best interest of the client, consistent with the applicable codes of ethics and laws, and in providing supervision in accord with the supervision guidelines. There are several legal theories of liability through which a client can proceed against the practitioner providing the direct service and the supervisor supervising the practitioner. These theories of liability and the elements required to be met therein vary by state. Claims made against the supervisor are generally secondary to those claims against the supervisee.

Direct and Indirect Liability in Supervision and Related Considerations

Supervision Guidelines

Most licensing boards and professional organizations have specific guidelines for supervision that set forth the requirements for supervisor qualifications and responsibilities as well as supervisee qualifications and responsibilities. It is important to note that any such applicable guidelines will be admissible in a court action to show the minimum standard of care or whether a supervisee or supervisor has breached his or her duty to the client.

Liability

Generally, a legal obligation, monetary or otherwise, that a practitioner or supervisor has incurred or may incur as a result of a negligent act and/or malpractice of the practitioner, supervisee, or supervisor.

Direct Liability

Practitioners or supervisees can be held directly liable for their own negligent acts in a malpractice action. Supervisors also can be held directly liable for their own acts in the supervision of a supervisee under the theories of negligent hiring or negligent supervision.

Malpractice

In the clinical context, malpractice is a form of negligence that requires four specific elements to be met. Essentially, in order to prove a case of negligence, the plaintiff must show that at the time of the alleged negligent incident, a legal duty between the practitioner and the client existed, the practitioner breached that duty, and that the client suffered harm or injury that was directly and proximately caused by the practitioner's breach of duty.

Negligent Supervision

Generally, in order to prove a case for negligent supervision, a plaintiff client must show that the supervisor failed to use ordinary care in supervising an employee by failing to prevent the supervisee's foreseeable misconduct and that there was a direct link between the supervisor's acts of commission or omission that resulted in injury to the client. For example, in *Simmons v. United States*, 805 F.2d 1363 (9th Cir. Wash 1986), the supervisor was informed of the sexual improprieties between his supervisee and his supervisee's client in January 1980, yet the supervisor failed to take any action and allowed the counseling relationship to continue until July 1981, which was found to cause psychological damages to the client. The court found that the supervisor was negligent in failing to take action to prevent further harm to the client and held the supervisor liable for damages that resulted from the negligent supervision. In a similar case, *Andrews v. United States*, 732 F.2d 366 (4th Cir. 1988), the court appeared to require an additional duty for the supervisor to investigate. In *Andrews*, the supervising physician knew of certain "sexual improprieties" of the supervisee and confronted the supervisee. At the supervisee's denial, the supervisor let the matter rest. As a result of the damages suffered by the plaintiff, liability was imposed on the supervisor for negligent supervision because he failed to sufficiently investigate the matter.

219

Negligent Hiring

Employers and universities have a responsibility to use reasonable care to determine if a prospective employee or student is unfit prior to hiring that student or placing that student in an agency setting. For example, if a university has knowledge that a student has a documented history of dangerous behavior and the university places that student at an agency site without disclosing the student's proclivity toward dangerousness, the university may be held liable for negligent hiring. Conversely, if the agency fails to ask whether the student being placed has a history of dangerous behavior before accepting that student for placement, the agency may be held liable for negligent hiring. In essence, in negligent hiring, liability is established on the basis of whether the university or employer had prior knowledge of the student's dangerous history.

Indirect Liability

Supervisees can be held indirectly or vicariously liable for the acts within the scope of employment of those they supervise even though the supervisor was not directly responsible for the injury. Vicarious liability is a legal concept, also known as "respondeat superior," which means "let the master answer." In terms of the supervision of students and unlicensed practitioners, in order to prove vicarious liability on the part of the supervisor, the plaintiff must show that a supervisory relationship between the supervisor and supervisee existed (by an employee-employer relationship, the borrowed servant rule, or enterprise liability), the supervisee was acting within the scope of employment, and that there was in fact an injury.

Employee-Employer Relationship

In determining whether an employee-employer relationship existed, the courts will look to a multitude of factors, such as whether the so-called employer, which in most cases will be an agency or university, had control over the firing and hiring of the supervisee, or whether the agency or university had any power to control the supervisees conduct. The actual exchange of remuneration for services, although one of the factors the court may consider, is not necessary to establish an employee-employer relationship.

Borrowed Servant Rule

In order to apply the Borrowed Servant Rule, there must be both a "master" or general employer and another employer, called a special employer, and only one shall be deemed the employer for purposes of liability. For example, in the context of a university training

220

program wherein a supervisee is under the supervision of both a university supervisor and a supervisor at an off-site agency, the university supervisor could be considered the master employer and the agency supervisor could be considered the special employer. This creates the possibility for the general or special employer to escape liability. In evaluating whether the general or special employer should be liable, the court will look to which party had the ability to control the supervisee at the time of the act.

Enterprise Liability
A legal theory wherein supervisor liability attaches when there is a factual determination that the supervisee's acts were a foreseeable risk of the enterprise. The application of this theory typically involves supervisors who charge clients for supervisee's services, potentially generating a profit. Theoretically, the benefits derived by the supervisor from the revenues generated from the supervisee's services are balanced by the risk of having to compensate an injured client. For example, in *Doe v. Samaritan Counseling Ctr.*, 791 P.2d 344 (Alas. 1990), the court concluded that the counseling center was liable for the sexual behavior of its practitioner employee toward a patient because it was "foreseeable" in light of the nature of the business and the transference phenomenon that the resulting sexual conduct was "incidental" to the therapy.

Scope of Employment
In determining whether the supervisee's acts fall within the scope of employment, courts will look to varying factors, such as the supervisor's power to control the supervisee, if the supervisee had a duty to perform the act, the time, place, and purpose of the supervisee's act, and the motivation of the supervisee in committing the act, but these factors are not always dispositive. For example, in *Simmons v. United States*, discussed earlier, a social worker engaged in sexually inappropriate behaviors with the client while on an out-of-town trip. The patient subsequently developed severe psychological problems as a result of the sexual relationship. The court found it immaterial that the sexual misconduct occurred outside of the usual time and place of the therapy relationship because the sexual relations were initiated during the therapy sessions. The sexual acts were within the course of employment because the wrongful conduct arose out of the therapy relationship.

Guidelines for Avoiding Direct and Indirect Liability in Supervision

- Both supervisors and supervisees must review what the code of ethics of the applicable professional organization and/or state or federal laws say about supervision and the particular requirements of the supervisor and supervisee.
- The supervisor should take all reasonable measures to ensure that the supervisee is aware of and abiding by the applicable code of ethics.
- The supervision should be performed on a formal basis and both the supervisor and the supervisee should document each supervision session and the implications thereof (i.e., changes in diagnosis, treatment plan, or intervention) in separate files.
- Supervisors and their supervisees are advised to meet on a frequent and regular basis.
- If a supervisee is supervised by both a university supervisor and an agency supervisor, there should be a contract with both that clearly details which entity will be in control of the supervisee and when.
- In cases in which supervisors are unclear as to how to proceed with a supervisee, supervisors should consider whether it would be helpful to seek consultation from trusted colleagues.

MALPRACTICE

Our society has become increasingly more litigious and, unfortunately, practitioners have been unable to escape the trend. Although malpractice suits are still relatively rare, practitioners must take action to protect themselves against malpractice. A lawsuit for malpractice is a civil suit brought by an aggrieved party, called the plaintiff, against the alleged tortfeasor, called the defendant, for monetary damages. In the clinical context, malpractice is a form of negligence that requires four specific elements to be met. Essentially, in order to prove a case of negligence, the plaintiff must show that, at the time of the alleged negligent incident or incidents, a legal duty between the practitioner and the client existed, the practitioner or supervisor breached that duty, and that the client suffered harm or injury that was directly and proximately caused by the practitioner's breach of duty. In some cases in which a clinical supervisor is supervising a practitioner working with a client, the aggrieved plaintiff sues the supervisor in conjunction with the practitioner or solely for malpractice, in which

222

case the supervisor may have indirect liability, or both the supervisor may have indirect liability and the practitioner may have direct liability for monetary damages to the plaintiff.

It is important for practitioners to remember that any client may bring a malpractice action against a practitioner and the practitioner is forced to defend himself or herself, regardless of whether liability is found. In other words, even groundless cases in which no liability is ever found are extremely expensive and tolling for the practitioner.

Malpractice and Related Considerations

Malpractice

In the clinical context, a form of negligence that requires four specific elements to be met. Essentially, in order to prove a case of negligence, the plaintiff must show that, at the time of the alleged negligent incident, a legal duty between the practitioner and the client existed, the practitioner breached that duty, and that the client suffered harm or injury that was directly and proximately caused by the practitioner's breach of duty.

Liability

Generally, a legal obligation, monetary or otherwise, that a practitioner or supervisor has incurred or may incur as a result of a negligent act and/or malpractice of the practitioner, supervisee, or supervisor.

Direct Liability

Practitioners or supervisees can be held directly liable for their own negligent acts in a malpractice action. Supervisors also can be held directly liable for their own acts in the supervision of a supervisee under the theories of negligent hiring or negligent supervision.

Indirect Liability

Supervisees can be held indirectly or vicariously liable for the acts within the scope of employment of those they supervise, even though the supervisor was not directly responsible for the injury. Vicarious liability is a legal concept, also known as "respondeat superior," which means "let the master answer." In terms of the supervision of students and unlicensed practitioners, in order to prove vicarious liability on the part of the supervisor, the plaintiff must show that a supervisory relationship between the supervisor and supervisee existed (by an employee-employer relationship, the

223

borrowed servant rule, or enterprise liability), the supervisee was acting within the scope of employment, and that there was in fact an injury.

Preponderance of the Evidence

The plaintiff has the legal burden of proof, that is, of proving each element of the asserted claim. In civil litigation, the burden of proof is preponderance of the evidence. Accordingly, in order to prove the defendant's liability, the plaintiff must prove each element by a preponderance of the evidence. A preponderance of the evidence is generally described as the greater weight of the evidence or more likely than not. For example, in a malpractice action, the plaintiff bears the burden of proof to show that it is more likely than not that the defendant had a duty to the plaintiff, that the defendant breached that duty, and that the defendant's breach of the duty was the direct and proximate cause of the plaintiff's damages.

Acts of Omission

Generally, acts of omission involve the practitioner not doing something that he or she should have done. Examples of acts of omission are not fully investigating a referral made to a client and not notifying the authorities when required by law such as in the case of mandatory reporting. Acts of omission may be just as serious as acts of commission.

Acts of Commission

Acts of commission occur when the practitioner affirmatively does something to breach the duty to the client. Examples of acts of commission are boundary violations, such as engaging in a sexual relationship with a client, and performing outside the scope of one's competence.

Malpractice and Insurance Coverage

Generally, liability is a legal obligation, monetary or otherwise, that a practitioner has incurred or may incur as a result of a negligent act and/ or malpractice of the practitioner. If the plaintiff is able to successfully prove all four elements by a preponderance of the evidence thereby proving liability, the defendant is ordered by the judge to pay money damages to the plaintiff. For those practitioners with malpractice insurance, the malpractice insurance carrier will usually provide legal defense counsel to represent the defendant practitioner and if the practitioner is found liable, the malpractice insurance carrier will pay the damages to the client. If the damages ordered to be paid exceed the insurance policy limits, the practitioner will be liable for any overage.

Settlement of Malpractice Claims

Very often, the litigants and/or the malpractice insurance carrier are able to resolve the malpractice action by entering into a settlement agreement and consequently, the case never proceeds to a trial verdict. A settlement can occur before a lawsuit is filed or as late as after trial but before the jury renders a verdict. Although the settlement agreement will commonly be confidential between the parties and their attorneys, even the result of a settled malpractice action can be devastating for a practitioner. The lawsuit and the allegations contained therein are public record and easily accessible by other clients, potential clients, and other professionals. Litigation and/or settlement negotiations are emotionally tolling for the practitioner and it is possible that other clients may suffer as a result of the alleged malpractice. Additionally, the malpractice insurance carrier will usually raise their rates significantly, even though liability was never established at trial.

Guidelines for Avoiding Malpractice Claims

- Practitioners must be aware of and abide by all applicable laws and codes of ethics in an effort to always practice competently.
- It is imperative for supervisors to take all reasonable measures to ensure that the supervisee is aware of and abiding by the applicable laws and codes of ethics.
- It is incumbent on practitioners to take each and every mention of a malpractice action seriously and make every effort to do damage control even where the practitioner believes the client has no basis for a malpractice claim.
- On receipt of a lawsuit of any kind, practitioners should contact their malpractice insurance carrier, and, if possible, retain an attorney to represent them and/or assist them in responding to the complaint.
- Practitioners should understand that it is normal to experience anxiety when served with a lawsuit.

225

- Once a lawsuit is filed against a practitioner, that practitioner should not speak to anyone about the lawsuit without an attorney representing that practitioner's interests present or without the consent of an attorney representing that practitioner's interests.

MANDATORY REPORTING

Practitioners are subject to mandatory reporting laws that serve the social function of protecting vulnerable groups. The legislators have created such laws with the acknowledgment that such vulnerable groups may be unable to protect themselves and require the protection of society as a whole and of professionals specifically. Such mandatory reporting laws require practitioners to report known or suspected physical and sexual abuse, neglect, and exploitation of persons in certain vulnerable groups in a timely manner. Although it varies by jurisdiction, vulnerable groups usually include children, elderly people who suffer from the infirmities of old age, and dependent or disabled adults. Most states do not indicate whether an instance of abuse is so remote in time to not trigger the mandatory reporting requirements. In other words, in those jurisdictions where the law is silent as to remoteness of suspected abuse, no matter how long ago, it should be reported by the practitioner. Mandatory reporting laws often create a dilemma for the practitioner because the practitioner is forced to balance the client's confidentiality against his or her social responsibility. Moreover, the information regarding the suspected abuse is not covered by the practitioner-client privilege. Practitioners must report suspected abuse when he or she has good reason, within the parameters of professional competence, to suspect that abuse is happening and does not generally require that the practitioner have proof of the abuse. In many states, a practitioner's failure to report suspected abuse would subject him or her to potential civil and criminal liability. When making a report, the practitioner will generally have to include the practitioner's name and address, the name and address of the suspected victim, and the nature of the suspected abuse. Most states will keep the reporter's identifying information confidential unless the case involves litigation. The practitioner's best defense to false allegations is to keep detailed accurate notes that include all statements and allegations made to the practitioner and the practitioner's statements made to the authorities.

Mandatory Reporting and Related Considerations

Confidentiality

The requirement, with some exceptions, that practitioners will not reveal to others the content of the information communicated by clients to them in therapy.

Practitioner-Client Privileged Communication

Practitioner-client privileged communication laws vary from state to state and the federal rule, but essentially all require, with some exceptions, that communications between a practitioner and a client are privileged and the practitioner cannot be forced to disclose such communications without the client's consent.

Mandatory Reporting Laws

Mandatory reporting laws require practitioners to report known or suspected vulnerable groups from physical and sexual abuse and exploitation in a timely manner.

"Good Faith" Mandatory Report

In general, a "good faith" report is one that is made by the practitioner without malice, based on professional counseling judgment.

Abuse (Adult)

Nonaccidental infliction of physical, sexual, social, or emotional harm or of economic exploitation of an adult Some jurisdictions require mandatory reporting of such actions for older adults, that is, those over the age of 65.

Abuse (Child)

Nonaccidental infliction of physical harm to a child, continual psychological damage, or denial of emotional needs (neglect).

Physical Abuse

Physical abuse generally involves an act that results in nonaccidental physical injury or trauma (i.e., punching, beating, kicking, biting, burning, or otherwise harming another) and often the physical injury is a result of unreasonable, severe corporal punishment or unjustifiable punishment.

227

Sexual Abuse
Sexual abuse usually includes sexual assault (i.e., rape, incest, sodomy, or oral copulation) and sexual exploitation (e.g., employment of a minor to perform obscene acts or assisting a child to engage in prostitution).

Exploitation
Exploitation can be sexually or monetarily oriented, but it usually involves the act of taking unjust advantage of another for one's own benefit. An example of financial exploitation of the elderly would be a caretaker hired to care for an elderly person who requires the elderly person to purchase her various expensive gifts as a condition to continued care.

Neglect
Neglect generally refers to the maltreatment, indication of harm, or threats to a vulnerable person's health or welfare by any person. Neglect will usually include both overt acts (i.e., deliberate starving) and omissions (i.e., failure to get proper medical attention).

Practitioner Immunity from Suit

When a practitioner makes a report of abuse without the client's consent, the practitioner may be sued and may even be found liable for the breach of confidentiality or defamation. The law in many states provides for absolute immunity from civil action for a practitioner who makes a good faith report of abuse or reports a reasonable suspicion that abuse has occurred. Many other states, however, simply impose the duty to report, without providing a concomitant immunity from civil liability for the reporter. When there is no statutory or case law provision for absolute privilege, courts generally extend a conditional or qualified privilege to report defamatory information where the reporter has a legal duty to do so. It is important to note, however, that any immunity would not protect the practitioner from being sued and having to defend an action.

Duty to Attempt Corroboration

When abuse is alleged, it must be reported, but is there an ongoing duty for the practitioner? Recent case law has suggested that there may, in fact, be an ongoing duty to attempt corroboration or independent verification if the allegation abuse is made by a child. In some jurisdictions, if the child continues to be seen, the practitioner has a duty to go beyond the client's words and look for corroborating evidence of abuse. It the child does not continue in therapy, the practitioner should document in the client record that corroborating evidence can not be obtained.

Guidelines for Mandatory Reporting

- Practitioners must know their state's mandatory reporting statute and learn which populations are considered vulnerable and the extent to which they are obligated to exercise their duty.
- Ensure that the practitioner's "Consent for Treatment" form clearly explains to the client the exceptions to confidentiality and the duty to report suspected child abuse, elder abuse, or abuse of disabled person to the state protection agency in that practitioner's jurisdiction.
- Practitioners need to take each and every suspicion of child abuse, elder abuse, or abuse of disabled person seriously.
- Is important for practitioners to keep in mind that they are only required to report suspected abuse and that they are not the actual fact finder who will make a final determination. The practitioner is only required to make a "good faith" report, which will be investigated by the appropriate authorities.
- When in doubt as to whether mandatory reporting has been triggered, practitioners should consider whether it would be helpful to seek supervision or consultation from trusted colleagues or legal counsel.
- If the suspected perpetrator is a current client, the practitioner should discuss with him or her the mandatory reporting requirement as indicated in your "Consent for Treatment" form, as long as there is no risk that further abuse or harm might come to the victim.
- If the suspected perpetrator is a current client and the treating practitioner makes the report of suspected abuse, the practitioner should attempt to convey to the client that the practitioner has an ongoing commitment to his or her welfare, notwithstanding the breach of confidentiality with the mandatory report.
- If appropriate and with the client's consent, the practitioner should continue counseling with the client or refer the client to a qualified practitioner for ongoing treatment.
- Practitioners must remember that abuse reporting can be an emotionally taxing experience and it is highly advised to seek the support of colleagues.

229

RECORD KEEPING

One of the most important responsibilities that a practitioner has is to keep adequate records regarding the diagnosis and treatment of each client. Three of the main purposes of client records are to ensure the quality of care for the client, document care for third-party reimbursement (i.e., managed care), and to protect the practitioner from potential client complaints and litigation. In general, a client record should contain identifying or intake information, assessment information (which may be in the form of a psychosocial assessment), treatment plans, progress or psychotherapy notes, and a termination note (which reviews the course of treatment and aftercare plan [i.e., referrals]). The Health Insurance Portability and Accountability Act of 1996 (HIPAA), fully implemented in April 2005, has created multiple obligations for practitioners in the handling of client's records, including informing the client of how their confidential records will be used and maintained, when and how it will be released to third parties, and how it will be accessible to the client. In general, the client is entitled to access, inspect, and copy his or her own client record unless the practitioner believes that it would be harmful for the client to do so. HIPAA has a requirement that distinguishes psychotherapy notes from other information in the client's records and mandates that psychotherapy notes be excluded from other elements of the client's record. Although the legislature varies from state to state, after terminating counseling with a client a practitioner should keep clinical records for a period of seven years, even in the event of a client's death. It is important to note, however, that in the case of clients who are under the age of majority at the time of counseling, the statutorily designated retention period (i.e., seven years) does not begin to run until the minor reaches the age of majority. When a practitioner does decide to destroy client records, the method of destruction must protect the client's confidentiality, such as by shredding or burning the client records.

Record Keeping and Related Considerations

HIPAA

The Health Insurance Portability and Accountability Act of 1996 (HIPAA) is federal legislation that requires organizations that provide or manage medical or psychotherapy services to be responsible and accountable for the policies and procedures used to protect client's records.

Psychotherapy Notes under HIPAA

HIPAA defines psychotherapy notes as those notes recorded by a practitioner that document or analyze a conversation with a client during a private, group, or family counseling session, excluding medication prescription information, session start and stop times, modalities and frequency of services, clinical test results, and any summaries of diagnosis, functional status, the treatment plan, symptoms, prognosis, and progress.

Psychosocial Assessment

A psychosocial assessment will generally contain the practitioner's assessment of the following areas of the client: psychological (i.e., motivation for treatment, cognitive ability), social and family relationships, recreational status, vocational/educational functioning, drug and alcohol use, and health.

Progress or Psychotherapy Notes

Progress or psychotherapy notes are written by the practitioner and document a client's progress, provide a record of events and interventions taken, and may serve as a means of communication among professionals working with the same client. Progress or psychotherapy notes are usually either problem-oriented, focusing on progress made in addressing the problem, or goal-oriented, focusing on progress made in reaching the treatment goal. Although the information contained in a progress or psychotherapy note is usually the same, there are a number of different formats a practitioner might use in drafting a progress note (usually known by their acronyms: DAP, SOAP, etc.).

SOAP Notes

A four section progress or psychotherapy note in which each letter of the acronym represents a section of the note: "S" contains the information given to the practitioner by the client during the session, "O" contains the factual information observed directly by the practitioner, "A" contains the practitioner's impression of the client, and "P" contains the plan for treatment and the practitioner's prognosis for the client.

Client Record Errors

When a client discovers a factual inaccuracy in his or her record the client has a right to request that the information be amended. The practitioner should ask for the request in writing and may ask for the specific reasons for the request. The practitioner then has a duty to investigate and if the

231

practitioner finds that an amendment is so warranted, then the information is amended. If the practitioner finds that a change is not warranted,
the client should be notified in writing of the denial and that he or she has
the right to submit a statement of disagreement, which will, if submitted,
become part of the client's record and will be released with the client's
protected health information as appropriate.

If the practitioner discovers an error in a client's record, the error
should be acknowledged and corrected by the person who made the error
by crossing one line through the error, inserting the corrected information, and initialing and dating the changes. The practitioner should notify
the client and any person or entity that received the inaccurate information of the changes made or of the statement of disagreement.

Client Records on the Death of the Practitioner

Practitioners continue to have the duty to safeguard and maintain client
records even after the practitioner's death. The practitioner has a responsibility to delineate in his or her estate plan how client files will be maintained. The intake form should state that in the event of the death of the
practitioner another practitioner of similar competence will take control
over the client records.

Client Records on the Death of the Client

A client's right to confidentiality continues even on the death of the client.
Although there are certain exceptions, HIPAA requires practitioners to act
as though a client's legal personal representative was actually the client
with regard to medical records and, accordingly, after the death of a client,
the client's personal representative is entitled to all of the client's records.

Guidelines for Record Keeping

- Practitioners must know the ethics codes, HIPAA, and legal statutes
  in their state or jurisdiction regarding the maintenance, storage, and
  dissemination of client records.
- Practitioners are encouraged to make a practice of documenting
  every session and/or interaction with each client.
- Practitioners should never change an entry in a client's record after
  the practitioner has written it without using proper protocol.

- Creating a backup copy of all client records is an effective way for practitioners to protect themselves.

- In the case of group, family, or couples counseling, each person in the group, family, or couple should have his or her own separate client record, which does not contain the identifying information of the other members of the group, family, or couple.

- Practitioners should maintain all client records at least the minimum time period required in their jurisdiction.

- Practitioners need to establish a plan for how their client's records will be handled on the practitioner's death.

- If a practitioner decides to destroy client records after the mandatory retention period, the practitioners should be sure to destroy the records in a manner that protects the client's confidentiality (i.e., shred or burn).

- Practitioners must follow all HIPAA requirements regarding safeguarding client files.

REPRESSED AND RECOVERED MEMORIES

The concept of repressed memories has recently garnered considerable attention and caused controversy. Although the term *repressed memories* is most commonly used in the media, courts, and legislature, some professionals have argued that the proper term is *dissociative amnesia*. Notwithstanding nomenclature, some practitioners believe that an experience, such as incest, is so traumatic that it may cause a client to repress memories of the actual event or events. Memory repression generally refers to the unconscious psychological process of storing a memory out of awareness because of the trauma connected with it. In many instances, people report recovering these repressed memories and can recall the actual event or events that were originally repressed. Generally, reports of recovered repressed memories are revealed in counseling for problems such as anxiety, depression, substance abuse, an inability to develop meaningful relationships, and/or sexual dysfunction.

Repressed and Recovered Memories and Related Considerations

Repressed Memory

A repressed memory is a memory, usually traumatic, of an event (or events) that is unconsciously psychologically stored outside the awareness of the conscious mind. There is an extensive amount of debate regarding the validity of repressed memories and accordingly, the idea that memories can be repressed and then recovered is not fully accepted in the counseling and psychology fields.

Recovered Memory

A recovered memory is that which was previously repressed and is now recovered and brought into consciousness years or decades after the event.

False Memory

A false memory is a memory of an event that did not happen or a memory of the distortion of an event that did occur.

Dissociative Amnesia

Classification 300.12 of the *Diagnostic and Statistical Manual of Mental Disorders—Fourth Edition* (*DSM-IV*) characterizes dissociative amnesia as an "inability to recall important personal information, usually of a traumatic or stressful nature, that is too extensive to be explained by ordinary forgetfulness." Clients with said diagnosis generally present with a retrospectively reported gap or series of gaps in memory for certain aspects of that client's history. The *DSM-IV* reports an increase in reported cases of Dissociative Amnesia, which involves previously "forgotten" early childhood traumas.

Repressed and Recovered Memories and Scientific and Technical Testimony

Over the past 25 years, there has been a rise in the number of cases in which repressed and recovered childhood memories play a pivotal role. As a result of recent amendments in legislation, victims with recently recalled memories of abuse may sue alleged perpetrators for events that happened years earlier. There has been in incredible amount of controversy over the veracity of recovered memories. As a result of the controversy, some courts have been hesitant to rely solely on evidence of recovered memories. Other courts, however, have readily accepted such testimony. Dissociative Amnesia, also referred to as repressed memories, appears in the *DSM-IV*, which was published by the American Psychiatric Association in 1994 and is currently the main diagnostic reference of mental health professionals in the United States of America. As a result of the recognition of dissociative amnesia in the *DSM-IV*, the concept of repressed memories has been generally accepted in the relevant scientific community and has satisfied courts following both the *Frye* Test and the *Daubert* Standard regarding the admissibility of scientific testimony into evidence in court.

Litigation against Practitioners Regarding Repressed and Recovered Memories

Practitioners are at risk for liability with regard to repressed and recovered memories. Unfortunately, the number of cases filed against practitioners for encouraging repressed and recovered memories and implanting false memories with clients has risen. Not all experts agree that traumatic memories can be repressed and subsequently recovered. In fact, some experts claim that reports of recovered memories are actually false. There is a strong body of research that suggests that it is possible for a practitioner to implant false memories. When a client appears in counseling with the common symptoms of childhood sexual abuse without actually reporting the occurrence of sexual abuse causing the client to experience false recovered memories, the practitioner naturally suspects childhood sexual abuse. Accordingly, the practitioner may begin probing for additional signs of childhood sexual abuse, even though the client has no memories of such instances. The practitioner's probes may prove suggestive to the client and can trigger the formation of false memories. Some false memories also may be induced by practitioners informing patients that certain symptoms indicate abuse and aggressively helping patients to "remember" such events. For example, in the case of *Rutherford, et al. v. Strand, et al.*, the Rutherfords and their children brought a lawsuit against Donna Strand, a psychological counselor at Park Crest Village Assembly of God, Inc. and the Reverend Robert Strand, the pastor of said church, seeking monetary damages that the Rutherfords alleged resulted from false recovered memories implanted by Ms. Strand. The lawsuit alleged defamation, intentional interference with economic relationship, professional malpractice, negligence, negligent infliction of emotional distress, and intentional or reckless infliction of emotional distress. Therein, Donna Strand, a church counselor, helped Beth Rutherford to remember over the course of 64 therapy sessions that her father, an Assemblies of God minister, had regularly raped and sodomized her between the ages of 7 and 14 and that her mother sometimes helped him by holding her down. Under Ms. Strand's guidance, Rutherford developed memories of her father twice impregnating her and forcing her to abort the fetus herself with a coat hanger. The father had to resign from his post as a clergyman when the allegations were made public. Later medical examination of Ms. Rutherford revealed, however, that she was still a virgin at age 22 and had never been pregnant. The family settled the lawsuit for $1 million.

Generally, a third party is not able bring a malpractice claim against a practitioner; however, there have been exceptions with regard to repressed and recovered memories. For example, in *Ramona v. Isabella*, No. 61898 (Cal. Super. Ct. May 13, 1994), the trial court permitted a California jury to find that the practitioners breached their duty of care to a third party, Mr. Ramona, when they treated his daughter, Holly, and encouraged her belief in her recovered memories of sexual abuse by her father, which was later determined to be untrue. The court found the practitioner liable for Mr. Ramona's monumental losses to his reputation, marriage, family life, and career. The *Ramona* Court reasoned that although it will not prevent all false claims and can not restore the integrity of the falsely accused, this judgment may deter false implantation and encourage the innocent to fight back.

Overall, it is imperative that practitioners make an extra effort to keep detailed documentation of clients who recover memories of traumatic events and when possible, request consent from the client to videotape sessions. The videotaped session may serve as the practitioner's best ally in defending a lawsuit that alleges that the practitioner implanted or created false memories.

Guidelines for Dealing with Repressed and Recovered Memories

- Practitioners need to know their state's mandatory reporting statutes and learn which populations are considered vulnerable and the extent to which practitioners are obligated to exercise their duty.
- Practitioners should take each and every allegation of abuse seriously.
- It is important for practitioners to keep in mind that they are only required to report suspected abuse and that they are not the actual fact finder who will make a final determination. The practitioner is

only required to make a "good faith" report, which will be investigated by the appropriate authorities.

- When in doubt as to whether mandatory reporting has been triggered, practitioners should consider whether it would be helpful to seek supervision or consultation from trusted colleagues or legal counsel.
- Practitioners are advised to take extreme precautions not to influence a client's recollection or lack thereof regarding an abuse history.
- Practitioners should avoid leading questions regarding childhood abuse.
- It is important for practitioners to make an extra effort to keep detailed documentation of clients who recover memories of traumatic events and, when possible, request consent from the client to videotape sessions.
- Working with abuse survivors can be an emotionally taxing experience, and it is highly advised to practitioners to seek the support of colleagues.

SEXUAL MISCONDUCT

Psychotherapy is often referred to as "the talking cure," so named because in counseling and therapy the client relates his or her innermost thoughts and feelings to a practitioner and through self-disclosure and working with the practitioner comes to know and understand himself or herself better. Self-disclosure may be essential for the client to resolve the issues for which he or she sought therapy. Client self-disclosure, however, also increases the power imbalance in the relationship, increasing the practitioner's power and decreasing the client's power, that is, power differential. The client may feel as though the practitioner is the first person who really listens or cares. The intimate connection involved in the practitioner-client relationship can bring about remarkable positive change if boundaries are maintained and the client's trust in the practitioner is not violated. Unfortunately, the most significant and positive features of the practitioner-client relationship also can be the most dangerous. Sometimes practitioners violate boundaries and the very issues that initially caused the client to seek the practitioner's services make him or her more vulnerable to victimization. When the practitioner violates boundaries and breaches his or her duty to the client by engaging in sexual misconduct or a sexual boundary violation, the adverse consequences to the client are tremendous. Sexual misconduct is considered one of the most serious breaches of the client's trust and a violation of client-practitioner boundaries.

Sexual Misconduct and Related Considerations

Sexual Misconduct
Any physical act of a sexual nature perpetrated against an individual without consent or when an individual is unable to freely give consent. It encompasses a range of behaviors, from inappropriate touching to rape. It also includes sexual exploitation.

Sexual Exploitation
The taking of nonconsensual, unjust sexual advantage of another for one's benefit or the benefit of another party. Such an act may or may not be accompanied by the use of coercion, intimidation, or through advantage gained by the use of alcohol or other drugs.

Sexual Misconduct in a Professional Relationship
The crossing of an appropriate sexual boundary with a client in violation of the practitioner's Code of Professional Ethics and/or legal statutes to which the practitioner is subject.

Power Differential
In a counseling context, the innate differential of influence favoring the practitioner in practitioner-client relationships, which can be either beneficial or harmful to the client.

Malpractice
In the clinical context, malpractice is a form of negligence that requires four specific elements to be met. Essentially, in order to prove a case of negligence, the plaintiff must show that, at the time of the alleged negligent incident or incidents, a legal duty between the practitioner and the client existed, the practitioner breached that duty, and that the client suffered harm or injury that was directly and proximately caused by the practitioner's breach of duty.

Liability
Generally, liability is a legal obligation, monetary or otherwise, that a practitioner or supervisor has incurred or may incur as a result of a negligent act and/or malpractice of the practitioner, supervisee, or supervisor.

238

Dual or Multiple Relationship
Dual relationships involve both a professional role and relationship, such as that of the practitioner, alongside a personal, social, business, or other nonprofessional role and relationship, such as a sexual partner. A multiple relationship is a term used to describe two or more types of relationships between a practitioner and a client.

Conflict of Interest
Conflict between loyalties or duties to a client or multiple roles with a single client. A conflict of interest arises when a practitioner has competing interests that interfere with faithfully exercising his/her professional judgment and skill in working with clients. It also can arise when the supervisor has competing interests that may interfere with the supervisor's duty to faithfully exercise his or her professional judgment in working with the supervisee.

Slippery Slope
Argument that a certain course of action will eventually lead to the erosion of all moral restraint. In counseling or therapeutic settings, it is the belief that small "innocent" boundary crossings will eventually result in gross, exploitive ones, such as sexual misconduct with clients.

Dynamics and Impact of Sexual Misconduct

Some distinguish various types or degrees of sexual misconduct such as sexual impropriety, sexual transgression, and sexual violation. Sexual impropriety is the lowest level of misconduct, nonphysical contact of a client that is disrespectful in manner and sexually demeaning. This includes inappropriate jokes, crude gestures, printed and posted sexual or double meaning cartoons or stories, or inappropriate comments about an individual's undergarments. Sexual transgression is the inappropriate touching of a client stopping just short of an overt sexual act. Sexual violation is the highest level of misconduct as it involves a sexual act between client and practitioner. There is no distinction between which party initiated the contact or whether the act was consensual.

It is generally accepted that sexual boundary violations create an unhealthy dual or multiple relationship between the client and the practitioner and are always harmful to the client. The ethical codes of every major professional organization for the helping professions specifically prohibit sexual relationships with clients. Sexual boundary violations involve the exploitation of the power differential between the practitioner and the client, typically occurring over the course of time as opposed to a spontaneous act by the practitioner in response to an irresistible urge. Sexual misconduct may occur in many different forms and is not just limited to sexual intercourse. It may occur when a practitioner self-discloses to a client personal, intimate, or private sexual feelings, fantasies or acts, or a specific sexual attraction to that client. Sexual misconduct also occurs when a practitioner makes sexual innuendos or suggestive comments about the client's body, attire, or appearance. Extreme forms of sexual misconduct are sexual transgressions when a practitioner holds, hugs, or comforts the client in such a way that the practitioner's needs are getting met as opposed to the client's needs. The most extreme is sexual violation wherein a practitioner engages in sexual intercourse or other sexual act with a client. Although not strictly prohibited, in some cases practitioner sexual misconduct can occur when a practitioner engages in a sexual relationship with a client's relative. In short, sexual misconduct with a client is ethically, legally, and criminally wrong.

No therapeutic approach orientation or training program that prepares mental health providers permits sexual contact with clients. Furthermore, the research literature consistently demonstrates that practitioner violation of sexual boundaries has a profound and long-term harm to clients. Nevertheless, sexual misconduct continues to negatively impact therapeutic relationships and causes physical and psychological damage.

The profile of practitioners who engage in sexual misconduct varies considerably. It ranges from those who engage in a single act of misconduct presumably because they are lonely, are having relational problems with a significant other, or have recently experienced a major loss, to those who are sexual predators and engage in ongoing sexual impropriety with multiple clients. Like other boundary violations, sexual misconduct is unlikely to happen quickly. Rather, it tends to be a process in which professional boundaries, including sexual ones, are increasingly stretched over time. This can include the practitioner's self-disclosure of his or her longing or dissatisfaction with a significant other, comments about the client's attractiveness or feelings toward her or him, extending length of sessions, suggesting meetings outside of scheduled appointments, and the like.

The practitioner may be subject to severe consequences for sexual misconduct, not only the discipline or suspension from applicable professional associations and licensing boards but also civil liability for malpractice. The victim will usually easily establish that the practitioner had a duty to the client, that sex in the therapeutic relationship is a breach of that duty, and that, as a result of that breach, the victim suffered injuries.

A final consideration is whether an intimate relationship with a client is ever possible after therapy has been terminated. This is a controversial issues in that some scholars and at least one professional code of ethics (the American Counseling Association) and even state statutes "permit" intimate relationships following the termination of therapy, usually at least two years. However, the permissive language of such codes or statutes was not meant to provide blanket permission for romantic or sexual relationships but, rather, to ensure that the practitioner would still have the responsibility to ensure that no harm befalls the former client. Thus, factors such as the extent of dependency the former client has for that practitioner, issues of the client's past relational difficulties and attachment style, and type of and duration of time since termination are critical in considering whether such a relationship could be harmful to the former client. The maxim "once a client, always a client" is worth pondering.

Guidelines for Avoiding Sexual Misconduct

- Practitioners should review the code of ethics of their professional association and/or state or federal laws.
- It is recommended that practitioners maintain an ongoing awareness of power differentials in the therapeutic relationship and the potential effects that power differential may have on the client.
- Practitioners should make a practice of assessing what other influences might be operative in their ethical decision making at the time, such as personal, relational or family problems, or social isolation or loneliness.
- Practitioners are advised to practice self care strategies regularly and consistently, especially during times of stress in their own personal life, as a way of reducing the risk of boundary violations with clients.
- Practitioners should consider whether it would be helpful to seek supervision or consultation from trusted colleagues about a particular situation that involves a potential sexual boundary violation.
- If posttermination intimate relationships with former clients are allowed by a practitioner's professional code and/or state statute, that practitioner should carefully consider factors that might

indicate that relationships could be harmful to the former clients. These factors include the individual's dependency on the practitioner, his or her past relational and attachment difficulties, the way in which therapy ended, and extent to which the power differential has shifted toward equality.

SUBPOENAS, RESPONDING TO

Receiving a subpoena of any kind is an anxiety-provoking event for most practitioners. Subpoenas generally require the person being served with the subpoena to respond in some fashion. Practitioners should not answer any questions, produce any records, or appear at a deposition or hearing without first consulting an attorney. The attorney will assess whether the subpoena is in fact valid and if it is valid will advise the practitioner how to respond. The attorney may file a motion for a protective order or a motion to quash or suppress the subpoena, either of which, if granted, will exempt the practitioner from responding or testifying. If the attorney advises that the records must be produced, some states have legislation that permits practitioners to produce only a written summary of the case rather than the client's entire record. If a practitioner does have to testify at a court proceeding or trial, the attorney should prepare the practitioner to testify and only those qualified as an expert are expected to give a professional opinion.

Responding to Subpoenas and Related Considerations

Subpoena
A legal document initiated by the judge—or, in some cases, an attorney—which requires the person being served with the subpoena to respond to interrogatories, or appear at a deposition or in court at a specified time, place, and date.

Subpoena *Duces Tecum*
A legal document initiated by the judge—or, in some cases, an attorney—which requires the person being served with the subpoena to appear at a deposition or in court at a specified time, place, and date with a specific set of records which are requested directly on the subpoenas *duces tecum*.

Interrogatory

A method of discovery or gathering relevant information whereby attorneys either issue a subpoena or request that the court issue a subpoena that requires the person being served to provide an answer or answers to a written question or questions under oath. Most states have limits on the number and type of interrogatories to which the practitioner can be required to answer. Practitioners should have an attorney review all written answers before responding.

Deposition

A deposition is a method of discovery or gathering relevant information whereby attorneys either issue a subpoena or request that the court issue a subpoena that requires a deponent to appear at a specified time, place, and date for questioning by the attorneys on both sides of the deponent under oath, all of which will be recorded by a court reporter.

Confidentiality

The requirement that practitioners will not reveal to others the content of the information communicated by clients to them in therapy.

Practitioner-Client Privileged Communication

Practitioner-client privileged communication laws vary from state to state and the federal rule, but essentially all require, with some exceptions, that communications between a practitioner and a client are privileged and the practitioner cannot be forced to disclose such communications without the client's consent.

Subpoenas and Confidentiality

A subpoena to appear for a deposition or to produce documents does not remove the practitioner's requirement and duty to keep the client's communications and records confidential. A practitioner, on receipt of a subpoena and after consultation with an attorney, should contact the client and ask the client for his or her written consent to waive the practitioner-client privilege. The client is the holder of the privilege and does not have to waive his or her right to confidentiality; however, often the client wants to waive the privilege, such as when the client is the plaintiff in a personal injury suit and requests that the practitioner testify as to the client's pain and suffering. If the client does not consent to waive the privilege, the practitioner may not disclose any privileged communications unless an exception to the privilege exists or a court order requiring disclosure is obtained.

Subpoenas and Client Records

In response to a subpoena *duces tecum*, practitioners should never produce an original record and, if producing anything at all, should be sure only to send that which is directly responsive to the subpoena and authored by that practitioner. Additionally, when appearing at a deposition or in court, the practitioner should not bring client records that have not been previously produced or requested. Finally, if a client record contains information about another client, that information should be deleted from the record before it is produced.

Payment for Services Responsive to a Subpoena

Generally, unless the practitioner has a provision in his or her informed consent document that requires a client reimburse the practitioner for time and expenses incurred in responding to a subpoena, a practitioner will have no means through which to recoup the costs of responding to a subpoena. Some states will allow a practitioner to condition production of requested documents on payment in advance of the reasonable cost of copies.

Guidelines for Responding to Subpoenas

- On receipt of a subpoena of any kind, practitioners should contact and if possible, retain an attorney to represent them and/or assist them in responding to the subpoena.
- Practitioners need to understand that it is normal to experience anxiety when served with a subpoena.
- If a practitioner receives a subpoena of any kind about a particular client, the practitioner should contact the client about whom the practitioner has been subpoenaed and ask that client for consent to appear at the deposition and/or release confidential information or records.
- If the client agrees to waive his or her privilege, obtain the necessary written consent.
- Practitioners should review the state and local rules regarding subpoenas, that is, type of information required to be produced. Generally speaking, this information can be obtained at the local library.

- If an attorney advises a practitioner to answer interrogatories, the practitioner should have the attorney review the answers before providing them to opposing counsel.
- If an attorney advises a practitioner to produce records, the practitioner should allow the attorney to review the documents before producing them and then send copies only of those documents directly responsive to the subpoena.
- If an attorney advises a practitioner to attend a deposition or testify in court and the practitioner's client has not waived the practitioner-client privilege, without a court order, the practitioner can only answer those questions that do not require revealing confidential communications from the client.
- If an attorney advises a practitioner to attend a deposition or testify in court and the practitioner's client consents to waive the practitioner-client privilege, the practitioner should answer all questions honestly, succinctly, and directly.

TERMINATING COUNSELING/THERAPY

Closure is important for many clients. When a client meets his or her goals in counseling or therapy or when the client no longer seems to be benefiting from counseling or therapy, termination is usually indicated. Ideally, the termination of counseling or therapy should be a collaborative decision whereby the practitioner and the client mutually agree on a time for termination, participate in a final exit counseling session, and establish necessary referrals, if any. Other ways in which counseling or therapy is terminated are when a client ceases all contact by failing to keep appointments or return calls and the practitioner is forced to terminate, when the practitioner believes the client is no longer benefiting from counseling or therapy and is ethically required to terminate counseling or therapy, when the client informs the practitioner of the intent to discontinue counseling or therapy, when a child's parent revokes consent for the practitioner to continue seeing the child, when the client is delinquent in payments to the practitioner and the practitioner terminates counseling or therapy, or when a managed care company decides that it will no longer pay for the client's sessions and the client will not or can not self pay for sessions. Although the laws regarding termination vary by state, at a minimum, in each case the practitioner should inform the client of the reason for termination, be sure not to abandon the client, and make the appropriate referrals.

Terminating Counseling/Therapy and Related Considerations

Termination

Termination is defined as the formal end to the therapeutic relationship between a practitioner and a client. Termination could be voluntary, such as when clients decide that they no longer want to participate in counseling, or involuntary, such as when a practitioner decides to terminate the relationship because the client is not progressing in counseling.

Documenting Termination

A practitioner should appropriately document a client's termination from counseling or therapy in the client's records by indicating the reason for the termination (i.e., treatment goals met or revocation of consent from parent) and, if recommended, any referrals for continuing treatment. It is particularly important for practitioners to document in the client's record when the practitioner believes that the client is not ready for termination or when the client is terminating against clinical advice. A letter of termination should be prepared and provided to the client.

Administrative Case Closure

When a client fails to appear for sessions, the practitioner must administratively close the client's case. In such situations, the practitioner should indicate the reason for the administrative case closure (i.e., client no longer attends scheduled sessions). A letter of termination can serve as the necessary documentation to terminate the relationship where the practitioner no longer has contact with the client and the practitioner wants to advise the client that the relationship is terminated.

Letter of Termination

A letter of termination is an effective tool to provide closure to the client, to serve as the written record of termination in the client's record, and to protect the practitioner from liability that could result from inappropriate client termination. A letter of termination may include the practitioner's recommendations for follow-up treatment, if any, the practitioner's availability to the client in the future if services are needed, and a notice that the client's file is available to either the client or, with the client's written consent, any other professionals who may need it. A letter of termination can be presented to the client in the client's exit session or can be mailed to the client who just fails to appear for sessions.

Delaying Termination

Most professional codes of ethics require termination when the client is no longer benefiting from therapy or when all treatment goals have been met. Unfortunately, some practitioners may continue counseling with a client even where the client is no longer benefiting from therapy. One reason may be the financial gain of ongoing therapy. In essence, the practitioner loses income each time a client terminates. Another reason a practitioner may continue therapy after the client is no longer benefiting is to satisfy his or her own emotional needs. It is imperative for practitioners to employ self-care strategies to avoid unnecessarily prolonging treatment.

Termination and Managed Care

Working in a managed care environment presents particular challenges for practitioners with regard to termination. Typically, a managed care company will limit participants to a maximum of number of sessions per year. Unfortunately for some clients, the managed care company will not always authorize the use of all available sessions. The managed care company will engage in the utilization review process, wherein the practitioner is required to contact the managed care company every few sessions to discuss the client's progress and the managed care company will then decide whether additional sessions are approved. The practitioner has a responsibility to continually prepare the client for the possibility of termination, not because the client is ready or is no longer benefiting from counseling, but because additional sessions may not be authorized by the managed care company. Practitioners are obligated to advise clients that the request for additional sessions may not be granted and unless the client can and will self-pay, counseling or therapy will be terminated. In a sense, the practitioner and the managed care client are forced to hope for the authorization of additional sessions but prepare for termination caused by the denial of additional sessions.

Termination and Referrals

If termination is necessary for any reason and the practitioner believes that additional treatment is necessary, the practitioner should provide the client with multiple referrals to professionals or agencies that are accessible and affordable for the client. The practitioner should also be sure that the professional or agency to which the client is referred has the capability of treating the client. Examples of inappropriate referrals are the client who was referred for an eating disorder to an agency that does not treat eating disorders or an indigent client who was referred to a facility that only accepts clients who can afford to privately pay for treatment. Practitioners can be held liable for a negligent referral when the practitioner made an inappropriate or harmful referral because of the practitioner's failure to investigate the professional or agency to which the client was referred.

Abandonment

Abandonment occurs when a practitioner inappropriately ends needed counseling with a client without giving the client adequate notice or time to prepare for the end of the relationship. When a client is abandoned, he or she feels trauma, anxiety, depression, or some form of being unsettled. Most professional organizations require practitioners not to abandon clients. When possible, practitioners need to prepare in advance of termination to avoid having the client feel abandoned. This, however, is not always possible. For example, when a parent revokes consent for a practitioner to continue seeing a child in counseling, the practitioner may not have prepared the child for termination. The child may have a sense of abandonment and the practitioner has no ability to help the child resolve his or her feelings of abandonment because the parent revoked consent for the practitioner to see the child.

Terminating Counseling/Therapy Guidelines

- Practitioners must know the ethics codes and legal statutes in their state or jurisdiction regarding terminating counseling or therapy.
- Practitioners must include in their informed consent document that the practitioner has the ability to terminate the relationship when, in the practitioner's opinion, the client is no longer progressing in counseling or therapy.
- It is important that practitioners continually monitor client progress to determine whether counseling or therapy continues to be beneficial to the client and, when it is not, take appropriate steps to terminate counseling or therapy.
- Practitioners need to document in the client's record the client's termination from counseling or therapy, the reason for the termination, and any referrals made.
- Practitioners are obliged to keep the client receiving therapy or counseling by payment from a managed care company advised regarding the managed care company's policy regarding session authorization.
- Practitioners are advised to make well-researched referrals to professionals or agencies that have the capability of treating the client and for which the client has the resources to access.

TESTIMONIAL PRIVILEGE

In the landmark case *Jaffee v. Redmond* , the U.S. Supreme Court established a practitioner-patient privilege under federal common law. The *Jaffee* Court held that "confidential communications between a licensed psychotherapist and her patients in the course of diagnosis or treatment are protected from compelled disclosure under Rule 501 of the Federal Rules of Evidence." Likewise, most states have a statute that requires the communications between the practitioner and the client be free from forced disclosure. Practitioner-client privileged communication or testimonial privilege laws vary from state to state and the federal rule, but essentially all require, with some exceptions, that communications between a practitioner and a client are privileged and the practitioner cannot be forced to disclose such communications without the client's consent.

In general, the client is the holder of the privilege and does not have to waive his or her right to confidentiality. In some cases, however, the client wants to waive the privilege, such as when the client is the plaintiff in a personal injury suit and requests that the practitioner testify as to the client's pain and suffering. If the client does not consent to waive the privilege, the practitioner may not disclose any privileged communications unless an exception to the privilege exists.

Testimonial Privilege and Related Considerations

Confidentiality
The requirement, with some exceptions, that practitioners will not reveal to others the content of the information communicated by clients to them in therapy.

Practitioner-Client Privileged Communication
Practitioner-client privileged communication laws vary from state to state and the federal rule, but essentially all require, with some exceptions, that communications between a practitioner and a client are privileged and the practitioner cannot be forced to disclose such communications without the client's consent.

Distinguishing Confidentiality and Privilege

It is important to note, however, that privilege and confidentiality are not interchangeable terms. Confidentiality is generally based on the client's right of privacy and on the oral or written contract between the practitioner and the client. Confidentiality belongs to both the practitioner and the client. Confidentiality has both ethical and legal implications for practitioners, but note, however, that without a testimonial privilege, a court may compel a practitioner to reveal confidential client information.

Privilege is generally based on state statute or the federal rule and is a purely legal concept. Privilege belongs exclusively to the client and only the client can chose to waive the privilege unless an exception to the testimonial privilege exists.

Exceptions to the Testimonial Privilege

It is widely recognized that there are exceptions to the practitioner's obligation of confidentiality to the client, such as when the duty to warn or the duty to protect is triggered or in the case of mandatory reporting. The exceptions to confidentiality generally require the practitioner to notify the appropriate parties (i.e., the police, the intended victim, the social services agency). The exceptions to confidentiality do not require the practitioner to testify about the client's confidential communications. It is important to note that there also may be exceptions to the testimonial privilege. The U.S. Courts of Appeals are split as to whether practitioners who breach confidentiality because of the duty to warn or duty to protect permits psychotherapists to testify about their otherwise confidential conversations with clients creating an exception to the testimonial privilege, or if it simply requires that they warn those individuals whom they deem to be in danger or those who can protect from the immediate danger. A recent California case, *United States v. Chase*, 301 F.3d 1019 (9th Cir. 2002), recognized a "dangerous patient" exception to the psychotherapist-patient federal evidentiary privilege that can be used to force practitioners to testify in criminal proceedings about their otherwise confidential communications with clients even when the client does not waive the testimonial privilege.

Guidelines for the Testimonial Privilege

- Practitioners need to know their state's testimonial privilege statute and any exceptions to it. Generally speaking, this information can be obtained at the local law library.
- Practitioners should ensure that the "Consent for Treatment" form clearly explains to the client the testimonial privilege and any potential exceptions to the privilege.
- When in doubt as to whether the testimonial privilege applies, practitioners should consider whether it would be helpful to seek supervision or consultation from trusted colleagues or legal counsel.

APPENDIX

Key Legal Cases and Legislation Impacting Mental Health Practice

Court rulings and legislative enactments have had a notable impact on mental health practice in the recent past and are likely to continue to influence practice patterns in the years to come. This appendix provides a very brief summary of court rulings and legislative enactments regarding a wide range of ethical and legal matters impacting the practice of mental health professionals. These thumbnail sketches only highlight the central finding or regulation. For further information on a case, the complete citation for each court ruling is provided. Topics are arranged by the following headings:

1. Cases Addressing Immunity from Liability in Breaching Confidentiality
2. Cases Addressing Duty to Warn/Duty to Protect
3. Cases Addressing Client-Practitioner Privileged Communication/ Confidentiality
4. Cases Addressing Liability in Clinical Supervision
5. Cases Addressing Negligence in Academic Advisement
6. Cases Addressing Mandatory Reporting
7. Cases Addressing Harassment
8. Cases Addressing Abortion Counseling
9. Cases Addressing School Curriculum
10. Cases Addressing ADHD
11. Cases Addressing Educational Placement
12. Legislation Influencing School Counseling Practice

1. CASES ADDRESSING IMMUNITY FROM LIABILITY IN BREACHING CONFIDENTIALITY

Wilkinson v. Balsaam

The court qualified immunity available under Vermont law and ruled that it did not apply due to the demonstrable presence of malice. [885 F.Supp. 651 (D.VT 1995) Vermont]

Krikorian v. Barry

Until a court throws the case out, mandated reporters still get sued, despite the absolute immunity. [1987; 196 Cal.App.3d 1211 (California)]

Stecks v. Young

Immunity is not necessary where the report is true; it is only necessary where the report is false. [1995; 38 Cal.App.4th 365]

Searcy v. Auerbach

A practitioner was wrong in contacting the child protective agency of another state to report an allegation of abuse from his client. The practitioner thought that he had immunity from prosecution under child reporting laws, but because the agency in his state was not informed, he was not covered by *his* state's immunity clause. Practitioners are only considered mandated reporters in the state in which they are licensed. [980 F.2d 609 (9th Cir. Federal Court 1992]

2. CASES ADDRESSING DUTY TO WARN/DUTY TO PROTECT

Tarasoff v. Regents of the University of California (1976)

When practitioners receive information that their client poses "a serious danger of violence to another" the practitioner must take steps "to protect the intended victim against such danger." [California Supreme Court: 17 Cal. 3d 425 131 Cal Rptr. 14, 551 p.2d 334 (1976)]

Hedlund v. Superior Court of Orange County

It is the practitioner's duty to warn family members potentially at risk from a client's violent acts. This extended the *Tarasoff* ruling by stating that merely failing to properly diagnose that a client was dangerous was a basis for liability. [Superior Court of Orange County, California: 34 Cal 3d 695, 669 P.2d 41, 45 (1983)]

Thompson v. County of Alameda

In the absence of a readily identifiable foreseeable victim, there was no duty to warn. Therefore a threat to a general *group* of potential victims does not create enough danger to warrant a duty to warn. [27 Cal. #d 741, 167 Cal. Rptr. 70, 614 P.2d 728 (1980)]

Ewing v. Goldstein

"Equally important information in the form of an actual threat that a parent shares with his or her son's therapist about the risk of grave bodily injury the patient poses to another also should be considered a 'patient communication' in determining whether the therapist's duty to warn is triggered." [2nd Dist., 2004 WL 1588240 (Cal. App. 2 Dist.) California (2004)]

Wilson v. Valley Mental Health

Court supported *Tarasoff* rule, but admitted concern that the statute "may inadvertently operate to create an incentive on the part of practitioners to avoid diagnostically appropriate examinations that could reveal specific threats and result in consequent duty to take preventative measures." [969 P.2d 416 Sup. Ct., Utah, (1998)].

Eisel v. Board of Education

A student told the school counselor that her friend intended to commit suicide. When the counselor spoke with the student who made the suicide statement, she denied ever making the comment. The counselor did not share the information with parents regarding the student's threat. Courts found that school personnel can be found liable if they fail to exercise "reasonable care" to prevent a student suicide as was determined in this case. In later proceedings, "reasonable care" was defined by the courts as taking each suicide threat seriously and taking precautions to protect the student including notifying the parents of the treat or risk of suicide. [1991, 597 A.2. 2d 447, Maryland]

Gathright v. Lincoln Insurance Co.

A third grade boy hung himself by a nylon cord in the school bathroom. The court decided that the school had taken adequate safety measures and that students cannot be sheltered from every possible danger whether self inflicted or otherwise. The school was not held liable. [(1985) 286 Ark. 16, 688 S.W.2d 931, Arkansas Supreme Court]

3. CASES ADDRESSING CLIENT-PRACTITIONER PRIVILEGED COMMUNICATION/CONFIDENTIALITY

Jaffee v. Redmond

U.S. Supreme Court upheld a lower court ruling that because all 50 states recognize some form of psychotherapist-patient privilege, that the Federal Rules of Evidence also (indirectly) recognize the same privilege. [US Supreme Court, 518 U.S. 1 (1996)]

United States v. Chase

U.S. 9th Circuit Court of Appeals decided that there was no dangerous person exemption to the federal psychotherapist-patient privilege, and that any breach of confidentiality because of a threat to others would be discharged by duty to warn statutes, but that such information would not be admissible at trial. [340 F.3d 978 (9th Cir. 2003)]

4. CASES ADDRESSING LIABILITY IN CLINICAL SUPERVISION

Tarasoff v. Regents of the University of California (1976)

In this case of a practitioner failing to sufficiently warn Tatiana Tarasoff that his client had threatened to kill her, the Supreme Court of California ruled that the practitioner's supervisor could be held liable because he had direct knowledge and control over the client's treatment. As a result of this, the supervisor assumed a duty of care for Ms. Tarasoff as if he were acting as the primary practitioner.

Altamonte v. New York Medical College (1994)

In this case, a supervisee, who revealed to a faculty member that he was a pedophile, sexually assaulted a child he was treating. The court held the educational institution was a supervisory institution and so was liable for supervisory negligence because it had a duty to the supervisee's client.

Andrews v. United States (1984)

A supervisor hears a complaint about sexual misconduct and confronts the supervisee whom denied the allegation after which the supervisor dropped the matter. The U.S. Court of Appeals found that the supervisor had been negligent in his duties because, although he had knowledge of allegations of sexual misconduct, he failed to sufficiently investigate the matter.

Simmons v. United States (1986)

An administrator expressed concern to a practitioner's supervisor about sexual impropriety with a client. The supervisor made no effort to take action. The court ruled that the supervisor was liable for negligent supervision for the attempted suicide, anxiety, and depression suffered by the client.

5. CASES ADDRESSING NEGLIGENCE IN ACADEMIC ADVISEMENT

Sain v. Cedar Rapids Community School District

A student was given erroneous advice by a school counselor resulting in the loss of an athletic scholarship. The loss was based on academic ineligibility as determined by the NCAA Clearinghouse. The Iowa Supreme Court found that school counselors must use care when advising students who need and rely on specific information such as courses and credits needed to pursue postsecondary endeavors. Stone (2002) presents this case and suggests the

2001 decision is a departure from the history of holding school counselors harmless and presents as a caution for practice. Stone (2002) also provides recommendations for the school counselor in their role as academic advisor and advocates for them to continue to embrace the role while exercising a good faith effort to give accurate advice. [(2001) 626 N.W. 2d 115, Iowa]

6. CASES ADDRESSING MANDATORY REPORTING

McDonald v. State

A teacher noted scratches on the neck of one of her students. The student told two versions of their origin: one of a kitten scratching her neck and another of her mother choking her, as the student also reported had happened on several occasions. The teacher consulted with the principal and child development specialist and a report was made to child welfare workers. The child was removed from the home. The allegations were unfounded and the parents brought suit against the teacher, the principal, and others. The courts decided the teacher and others involved acted in good faith and with reasonable cause to suspect child abuse and were granted immunity from the suit. Forty-nine states currently have mandatory reporting laws, many with clauses regarding immunity based on good faith and reasonable cause reporting. [(1985) 71 Or. App. 751, 694 P.2d 569, Oregon]

7. CASES ADDRESSING HARASSMENT

Davis v. Monroe County Board of Education

A fifth grade girl reported being tormented by a boy in her class. School officials were aware of the offensive nature and severity of the harassment but did not take any steps to remedy the on going problem. The U.S. Supreme Court determined that schools may be liable for peer-peer sexual harassment based on Title IX but only when acting with "deliberate indifference." [(1999), 562 U.S. 629, 119 S. Ct. 1661]

Wagner v. Fayetteville Public Schools

These administrative proceedings involving the Office of Civil rights of the U.S. Department of Education resulted when a school district failed to take meaningful action to prevent harassment based on sexual orientation and culminated in an agreement with the Fayetteville School District requiring the district to recognize harassment directed at gay and lesbian students, provide training for students and staff, and submit written reports monitoring progress. These proceedings were presented and discussed by McFarland and Dupuis (2001). [1998, Administrative Proceedings of the U.S. Department of Education]

Gerber v. Lago Vista Independent School District

This U.S. Supreme Court ruling found that schools (districts) can be held liable when teachers sexually harass students if an official of the school knows of the harassment and fails to take action. [1998, 524 U.S. 274, 118 S. Ct.]

8. CASES ADDRESSING ABORTION COUNSELING

Arnold v. Board of Education of Escambia County

Two students and their parents filed suit against the school district, stating that the school counselor had coerced and assisted the female student in getting an abortion, paid someone to drive the student to have the abortion, and provided paid tasks to the two students to earn money for the abortion. The courts found that the students were not deprived of their own free will, had chosen not to tell their parents, and were not coerced. During the trial, it was discovered that the school counselor had repeatedly encouraged the students to consult with their parents and presented various alternatives that were rejected by the students who admitted that the decision to obtain the abortion was theirs alone. Stone (2002) presents this case along with recommendations for school counselors. [(1989) 880 F. 2d 305, Alabama]

9. CASES ADDRESSING SCHOOL CURRICULUM

Leebaert v. Harrington

A father argued his right to direct the education of his son by requesting that his son be excused from health education classes in his public school that included discussions of drugs, sexual harassment, family life, and AIDS. Although the court acknowledged the importance of parents in the upbringing and education of their children, parents can not dictate or control the flow of information with regard to the curriculum of a public school to which they choose to send their child. [(2003) 332 F3d 134, U.S. Court of Appeals]

10. CASES ADDRESSING ADHD

W.B. v. Matula et al

The parent of an ADHD child filed suit claiming that school officials failed to properly evaluate, classify, and provide necessary educational services for the student. The case was initially dismissed then sent to the U.S. Court of Appeals, where the court ruled that there were violations of Section 504, IDEA, and constitutional rights based on the unwillingness of school personnel to recognize and accommodate the student's disability. [(1995) 67 F.3.d 484 (3rd Cir.)]

11. CASES ADDRESSING EDUCATIONAL PLACEMENT

Florence County School District v. Carter

The court decided that school authorities can be held responsible for reimbursing parents for expenditures on private education if the court finds that the student's educational placement is inappropriate and the parent's placement of their child in private school is appropriate. Congress has delineated what parents must do if they are to be reimbursed after withdrawing a child. [(1993) 510 U.S. 7, 114 S. Ct. 361, U.S. Supreme Court]

12. LEGISLATION INFLUENCING SCHOOL COUNSELING PRACTICE

Family Educational Rights and Privacy Act of 1974 (FERPA)

Also known as the Buckley Amendment, this law applies to all schools and districts that receive federal funds from the U.S. Department of

Education. It has provisions for parental review of student records, determining who may access records, determining what information can be disclosed from a student record without consent, and provides guidelines for counselors' "personal notes."

Free Appropriate Public Education (FAPE)

Under IDEA, all handicapped children have the right to a free appropriate public education (FAPE). FAPE has been defined as special education and related services that have been provided at public expense, under public supervision while meeting state standards, and are provided in conformity with the required IEP.

Individuals with Disabilities Education Act (IDEA)

In 1990, EAHCA (PL 94–142) was renamed the Individuals with Disabilities Education Act (IDEA, PL 101–476). Amendments to IDEA in 1997 affected several aspects of the statue (with implications for school counselors) including eligibility, evaluation, programming, discipline, and procedural safeguards. IDEA provides very specific procedures for providing a free and appropriate public education and applies only to education agencies that receive funds under IDEA.

Least Restrictive Environment (LRE)

To the maximum extent possible, students with disabilities are educated with students who are not disabled. Students with disabilities are removed from the regular classroom only when the severity of their disability is such that the use of supplementary aids and services in the regular classroom will not allow them to achieve satisfactorily.

Section 504 of the Rehabilitation Act of 1973

Section 504 deals particularly with students with disabilities seeking equal educational opportunities and applies to all public educational institutions. Section 504 students must have record of a physical or mental impairment that substantially limits one of their major life functions (such as seeing, walking, hearing, or attending school) and be regarded as having such impairment.

Individualized Education Plan (IEP)

An individual plan written for students reflecting their educational needs, instructional goals and objectives, and evaluation procedures that will help monitor student progress toward goals and objectives.

Americans with Disabilities Act of 1990 (ADA)

This act prohibits discrimination against individuals at work, in school, and in public accommodations. Schools must make reasonable accommodations for people with disabilities. This act is not limited to organizations receiving federal funds.

Education for All Handicapped Children Act of 1975 (EAHCA, also known as Public Law 94–142)

This legislation ensures the right of all students with disabilities to receive a free appropriate public education, special education and related services, an individualized education program, due process procedures, and the least restrictive environment in which to learn.

Rehabilitation Act of 1973

This act states that no handicapped person in the United States shall be excluded from participation, denied benefits, or be subject to discrimination based solely on their handicap. It pertains to any program or activity receiving federal financial assistance.

Section 504 Plan

An accommodation plan written for students who meet requirements under Section 504. Although the plan is similar to an Individualized Education Plan (IEP), Section 504 is not as specific as IDEA in regarding what shall be included in the plan.

INDEX